Let us now Praise Famous Women

Andrea Fisher is an American artist and writer who lives and works in London. She also Tutor in Fine Art and Cultural Criticism at Goldsmiths' College, University of London, and is working on her D.Phil at the University of Leeds. Andrea Fisher is Curator for the exhibition of photographs commissioned by the National Museum of Photography, Film and Television, UK, entitled *Let Us Now Praise Famous Women*, in which this book is based.

PANDORA PRESS

Let us now Praise Famous Women

Women Photographers for the US Government 1935 to 1944

Esther Bubley
Marjory Collins
Pauline Ehrlich
Dorothea Lange
Martha McMillan Roberts
Marion Post Wolcott
Ann Rosener
Louise Rosskam

Andrea Fisher

PANDORA
London and New York

First published in 1987 by
Pandora Press (Routledge & Kegan Paul Ltd)
11 New Fetter Lane, London EC4P 4EE

Published in the USA by
Pandora Press (Routledge & Kegan Paul Inc.)
in association with Methuen Inc.
29 West 35th Street, New York, NY 10001

Set in Palatino 11pt
by Butler & Tanner Ltd
and printed and bound in Great Britain
by Butler and Tanner Ltd
Frome and London

Library of Congress Cataloging in Publication Data

Let us now praise famous women.
1. Photography, documentary—United States—exhibitions.
2. Women photographers—United States—exhibitions.
3. United States—history—twentieth century—pictorial work—exhibitions.
4. Women photographers—United States—biography.
I. Fisher, Andrea, 1955–
TR820.5.L48   1987   779'.9973917   87–2544

ISBN 0 86358 123 4 (p)

Women Photographers for the US Government 1935 to 1944

Esther Bubley
Marjory Collins
Pauline Ehrlich
Dorothea Lange
Martha McMillan Roberts
Marion Post Wolcott
Ann Rosener
Louise Rosskam

Contents

Acknowledgments

I would like to warmly thank Tony Benn for his immeasurable support, both editorial and emotional. Esther Bubley, Martha McMillan and Marion Post Wolcott have been extremely generous in sharing their experience through extended conversations. Dr Griselda Pollock, at the University of Leeds, has been of invaluable help through her continued interest, guidance and criticism. I would like to thank Terry Morden, Exhibitions Organiser at the National Museum of Photography, Film and Television, for making possible the exhibition upon which this book is based. The work of John Tagg, co-curator of the exhibition, has of course been a key part of the project. Lastly, I would like to acknowledge the assistance of the staff at the Library of Congress Prints and Photographs Collection, and the Ledel Gallery in New York City, for their assistance in completing the research for this project.

A.F.

Introduction

To make present the work of women who have remained invisible in the writings of history is, in itself, only an opening on further questions. Such research invites reflection on their prior absence as a meaningful silence within the historical discourse that informs our own times. Of the eight women photographers represented in this volume, only two have been the subjects of prior historical writing. Yet it is not the simple fact of a woman's absence that incites our historical inquiry. The recovery of her work and the sudden recognition of her as an object of intrigue interrogates the process of our own fascinations: the relation between that woman's work and the disparate demands of the present. Her history is, then, no longer the disclosure of a lost and distant past; it is a relation, a writing and, thus, a production of our present.

Between 1935 and 1944, two U.S. Government agencies aimed to produce an encyclopedic record of American life through documentary photographs. Many of the photographers who contributed to this file have become prominent figures in the popular and permissible memory of that moment—among them, Walker Evans, Ben Shahn and Dorothea Lange. Yet of the eight women who took photographs for the Farm Security Administration and the Office of War Information, only Dorothea Lange and Marion Post Wolcott's work have become visible in the comtemporary writing of that past. And only select samples of Lange and Post Wolcott's photographs are repeatedly re-presented. In exclusivity, these few images have been taken as emblematic, not only of the photographers' larger œuvre but also of the period as a whole.

In addition to many little-known works by Dorothea Lange and Marion Post Wolcott, this volume presents the heretofore unexplored works of Esther Bubley, Marjory Collins, Pauline Ehrlich, Martha McMillan Roberts, Ann Rosener and Louise Rosskam, all of which were undertaken for these agencies. It also gathers together many of the books and periodicals in which the photographs gained wide circulation at the time of their production. The book accompanies a major exhibition, co-curated with John Tagg, launched by the National Museum of Photography, Film and Television in Bradford, U.K., in April 1987.

A single published image by Esther Bubley in Roy Stryker and Nancy Wood's *In This Proud Land* had prompted curiosity about the other unexplored works by women which might be waiting in the Washington files of the FSA and OWI. Successive periods of research brought to light this substantial body of work by six other women photographers. Not only are these images remarkable in their visual quality; many represent a dramatic shift in photographic approach away from the now familiar documents of the Depression. Scattered amongst the images of dustbowls and destitute migration were the highly sensuous urban subjects of the 1940s, marked by reverie and reminiscent of filmic narrative. It is only in this later period that most women entered the government's documentary agencies, producing images of quite a different kind: images which raise questions about our concept of documentary truth and the relation of women to it.

A number of studies have examined the FSA photographs as pictorial evidence of a bygone world. They have not addressed the photographs, however, but an imputed historical reality glimpsed beyond them. By treating the images as mere windows on the world, they implicitly trust the photograph as impartial evidence. Yet amongst the images produced by the women photographers, dramatic shifts appear, not only in the pictured world but also in their approach to picturing. From Lange's work in the mid-1930's to the work of Bubley, Collins and Rosener in the early 1940's, the practice of photography was transformed. Lange's was the classic documentarist's attempt at a transparent testament to the plight of migrant families, uprooted but, apparently, enduring the crisis. From her evenly lit agrarian expanses to the provocatively posed urban interiors produced during the 1940's, a new visual rhetoric had emerged. It was not merely the historical moment which had changed but the very means with which those moments could be grasped and understood.

The means with which the social could be known had been transformed; with this went concomitant changes in the means with which the personal could be spoken and understood: a re-ordering of the relation between the masculine and the feminine, the personal and the public, sexuality and the family. Such shifts became visible not only in the photographs themselves, but in the way the womanhood of each photographer was addressed and accepted in her time. In the endless speech seeking to identify the feminine, the identities of the women photographers and the readings of their work were continually redefined.

The following essay is concerned less with the biographies of individual photographers than with the terms in which each was made visible within her respective moment. The social crisis of the 1930's consisted not only in economic collapse, but equally in an uncertainty surrounding personal identity. At the centre of that uncertainty lay fractures and change in prevailing notions of the masculine and feminine. Amidst this troubling flux in the identity of gender, each woman photographer became a site at which a naming of the feminine might be publicly propounded and secured. Dorothea Lange and Marion Post Wolcott, in particular, were the objects of an insistent public discourse pertaining to their womanhood.

Yet beyond the intrigue of the past itself, the essay attempts to foreground the contemporary terms with which we construct that historical narrative. In the process of writing, the women photographers are again made visible. They are unavoidably written in the terms with which we speak, and attempt to know our present. The attempts during the 1930's to define the femininity of the photographers are inevitably recounted with the words we choose to speak of our contemporary feminine. And our fascination with such uncertainty surrounding the feminine speaks forcefully of our own tenuous hold on identity.

The essay addresses our desire for memory, and for the coherence of historical narrative: a dream of uniting all the lost fragments of our past, impelled by our fractured present. It addresses the seduction of those materials we summon from the past as a play of our present-day desire. It results not in a total knowledge of days gone by, but in a production in and of our present.

The Farm Security Administration was one of the most visible aspects of the New Deal: a comprehensive rosta of reforms enacted by the American government in response to the depth of the Depression. Three years after the stock market crash of 1929, apologists for President Hoover claimed that 'the battle against the Depression had been won'; yet evidence of that victory was scarce. City centers were scarred with breadlines, soup kitchens, and scores of half-built houses, factories and offices. On the outskirts of the cities, the scattered shanty towns were sarcasticly renamed "Hoovervilles." Shops and factories everywhere lay idle. Hundreds of thousands of farmers, who had lost their homes through forced sales, wandered the countryside in search of migratory rural work. During the winter of 1932–33 over 20% of the population was unemployed. From the nationally organized Hunger Marches to the farmers' spontaneous rebellions against foreclosures, widespread protest challenged the existing order.

The Depression penetrated the full network of economic and social institutions, and undermined the very bases of American national identity. In its severity, it shattered the shared belief that the existing system could continue to function equitably. Upon his presidential election in 1932, Franklin Delano Roosevelt responded to the crisis with the New Deal's sweeping legislation for relief and reform. Yet the purpose of the New Deal was not structural social change; rather, it aimed to seal a popular alliance which would support moves towards corporate recovery, concentration and renewed expansion.[1]

The New Deal effected a radical diffusion of the agencies of government throughout social, cultural and personal practise. As a presence which then permeated every aspect of social life, it hoped to quell the crisis in social identity. On one hand, the New Deal offered employment in public works, constructing roads and dams, schools and hospitals, clearing slums and replacing homes; it secured bargaining rights for the emergent and powerful industrial trade unions, curtailed the growth of trusts and cartels, and established minimum wages and maximum working hours; it enacted the country's first social security care for the elderly, disabled and needy. But, on the other hand, it equally affected private corporate and agricultural policy through its strategy for economic recovery. Its reach extended from the regulation of all central arenas of banking, commerce and communications, to the support of regional development and rural electrification, from the provision of camps for the migratory homeless to the construction of model farms.

Through its extension into such diverse fields, the boundaries of the state became diffuse; and in the intensity of the New Deal's impact on the lives of every American, he or she was summoned into a radically new contact with the nation. From coast to coast, each individual felt that impact; yet as recipients of aid rather than as agents of their own social change, each remained remote from any potential sense of the collective. In its penetration, the New Deal worked to reinstate a national identity, common from coast to coast, yet made safe from the perils of the communal, much less the potentially communist.

Within its bid to command the crisis in social identity, the cultural practices promoted by the New Deal held a privileged place. The work relief funding of 1935 established the Federal Arts Project, employing artists and designers, musicians and writers, and all those engaged in the theater arts to complete new works and open community arts centers in even the smallest towns across the country. The arts thus newly emerged as a truly national arena. As practices in representation, they assumed immense authority as an arena in which the crisis could be grasped and debated. Yet that debate was marked as much by its breadth as by its parameters; "unacceptable" projects were vetoed or destroyed. The Federal Arts Project emerges not only as a powerful site of debate but also as a site of the New Deal's power.

Within this cultural work, the documentary photography of the Farm Security Administration was equally pervasive. In response to the widespread destitution of farmers who had been driven off their land, the Resettlement Administration (later renamed the FSA) was set up in 1935 for resettlement and land use programs, construction of model communities and rural rehabilitation through loans and grants to purchase land, equipment and livestock. As head of the FSA's Historical Section, Roy Stryker set out to record photographically the rural crisis in order to persuade those in power of the necessity for the agency's work. Dorothea Lange and Marion Post Wolcott were amongst those hired to this end.

In their circulation throughout the nation's newspapers and journals, the resulting file of images signified a sectional need for rural relief as the crux of the national crisis, and a matter of national concern. In their vision, the rural poor were neither broken nor hopeless, neither derelicts nor drifters; rather, they stood as sturdy independent Americans, stricken by circumstance and merely in need of a temporary helping hand. The rural needy were thus conveyed to an urban audience: equal in their essential Americanness, yet deserving of sympathy in their dependence on the power of urban concern. In so doing, they secured a cohesive American identity, and a shared deference to the state as the sole means by which that proud resilience might be affirmed and reinstated.

Stryker remained with the FSA until the political tensions which threatened the New Deal finally prevailed. The United States' entry into the Second World War meant that his documentary project was transferred to the Office of War Information in 1941. It was during the latter days of the FSA and the period with the OWI that Esther Bubley, Marjory Collins, Pauline Ehrlich, Martha McMillan Roberts, Ann Rosener and Louise Rosskam contributed to the file.

The shifting terms in which the women photographers and their work were seen may themselves be understood as one site of the social crisis: a crisis that undermined both social and personal identity. "A Crisis of the Intimate" presents the 1930s social crisis as one which exceeded economics to penetrate the intimate arenas of sexuality and identity. The rift which had opened between experienced hardship and its minimal acknowledgment by both the government and media severed people's trust in established authorities and shattered the consensus around their portrayal of the social process. And where the social truth had been ruptured, the truth of personal identity within that social process was equally at risk. In relation to the women photographers, the uncertain identity of the feminine was signaled in a wealth of discourse pertaining to their gender.

This historical account, grounded as it must be in archival research, nonetheless recalls its partial truth. It draws a picture of the past from those remaining traces legible within our imperatives. It remembers a past and yet understands that memory as a longing to place the present: a longing to pinpoint our present location by casting that retrospective line behind us. It evokes a position of command over all that has transpired, and so promises the fiction of a singular knowing self. Yet it remains one writing set amongst others, and only one of several positions provoked by the photographs.

"Intensities in the Present" opens on the modern archive as the architectural space constructing our "discovery" of the photographs. Within it, history appears to be sealed and concealed as a distant and troubled past overcome by the plenitude of the present. Yet within the library, documents of the past intrude into our present and are placed within relations of contemporary power. The images incite the power of disengaged scholars over their object of study. And amid the flux of the modern city, the library attempts a fixed classification of knowledge. Its order stands out as a refusal of the uneasy differences at play within the present. The library emerges not as safe storage of our cherished traditions, but as a site of several relations of power.

"An Uncertain Exchange" recounts my meeting with Esther Bubley. Two women met over the body of her images, with which each had a powerful relation. Yet each found in those images an antithetical truth. It was not simply a schism caused by a sense of the images had made in the 1940s and the meaning we derive from them now. For we had spoken with one another in the present; and we exchanged with each other the disparate intensities incited by her pictures in the present. There was no truth about the images to be distilled from our meeting; no position of mastery to be attained. Our encounter was one of partial truths, and one which pointed to the folly of a final knowledge.

As we look at her images, we endlessly recreate their meanings; and with each meaning, we equally sense ourselves to be re-placed. Far from reflecting our cohesion, they become openings on the fragility of identity. As arenas for our engagement, the images are continually traversed by our fluid and fragmented desires.

"The Drift of Reverie" writes the intrigue of a single image. Fascination provokes our presence as inexhaustible unfolding: progression towards a position of knowledge, perpetually deferred. Through simultaneous readings, we fabricate Self as multiplicity. Our play of mastery falls away, and with it History as the coherent tale of our past.

Across the essay's four fragments, the images are re-drawn through a difference of desires: the difference that we are and that we make in writing. In their interrelation, such writings construct history as a play of difference, and make the present the dispersion that we are.

Note

1. Despite the formation of the nation's first work relief programs for the unemployed, several millions were left to fend for themselves. Even under the New Deal's largest relief appropriation, the Emergency Relief Appropriation Act of 1935, work was to be found only for 3.5 million jobless while the other 1.5 million on relief were considered chronic cases and consigned to the charity of private agencies.

   In relation to women many of the government's measures merely reinforced existing gender identities. Under the pressure of unemployment, the federal governments ruled in 1932 that only one spouse could be employed in public service. The double imperatives of maintaining the masculinity of the family breadwinner, and the higher wages normally earned by men, meant that it was invariably the women who stood down. And while working wages and hours were regulated under the New Deal's labor legislation, wage differentials between men and women were legalized at the same time.

   In contrast, both the New Deal's industrial and agricultural policies served to concentrate capital, adversely effecting many of the waged and small entrepreneurs in both fields. Agricultural policy enforced artificially high prices in exchange for reduced production, thus encouraging the big farmers to shed their tenant farmers and farm laborers.

The Photographers

☐ Where other texts have approached the period through the lives of individual photographers, I have sought to foreground the social terms which each assumed and transformed in their personal lives. But in that traversal of each intimate life by the public, it is nonetheless compelling to place the images, not only historically, but in the context of the lives comprising that history.

Across these eight lives there is less communality than diversity. Perhaps they shared only in that each was university educated, in either fine art or photography, and each was relatively new to her profession when she came to work with either the FSA or OWI. Having begun their careers at the moment of documentary's emergence as an idiom, they formed, in their subsequent work, the first generation of jobbing photographers: neither the individual visionaries of fine art nor the entrepreneurs of the private portrait studios. In the range and the public prominence of their work, they attest to the impact of the FSA and OWI documentary projects on wider photojournalistic practise.

Research thus far has revealed only fragments about the backgrounds and concerns of the lesser known photographers. The lives of Marjorie Collins, Ann Rosener and Pauline Ehrlich have sadly remained completely obscured. But, in addition to my archival research, I have been fortunate in having extended conversations, personally with Esther Bubley, and by telephone with Marion Post Wolcott and Martha McMillan Roberts. Esther Bubley told me of her university background in the arts and her apprenticeship as a photographer with *Vogue Magazine* before turning away from both art and fashion photography to become a dedicated documentarist. Though originally hired as a lab technician for the FSA, in 1941, she independently shot her first contributions to the file, and began receiving photographic assignments just as Stryker and the FSA Historical Section were being transferred to the Office of War Information. Though her OWI work has remained completely unknown, her subsequent work with Stryker for Standard Oil did achieve considerable notoriety, enabling her to proceed to *Life Magazine*, and to freelance after *Life*'s demise in 1972. She is currently planning a documentary book on the homeless in New York City.

Martha McMillan Roberts described her brief period with the FSA in 1941 as the "apprenticeship" which "taught me everything." She had come to the FSA directly from her study of art at the experimental Black Mountain College. Her assignments, in those last months of the FSA, were not to the rural poor but primarily to the monuments and pastimes of the capitol. Yet she shared energetically in the FSA's faith in reform and in governmental responsibility towards the people. At this stage in her career, however, she felt Stryker to be overly protective, particularly towards his female staff, and soon transferred to the newly formed Washington bureau of the *Chicago Sun Times* as their photographer, photo editor and administrator. Only when she returned to Stryker's employ in 1946, as an accomplished photographer with Standard Oil, did she feel she worked with him easily, producing extensive documents on the industry of the South. She has subsequently published her own book *Public Gardens and Arboretums of the United States*, photographed for the Kennedy administration's Commission on Youth, the United Mineworkers, the AFL-CIO, and has been published in such journals as *The Lamp, Fortune*, and *Women's Day*.

Edwin and Louise Rosskam, husband and wife, photographed as a team from their first professional appointment with the *Philadelphia Record* in 1936. Despite his training as a painter and her study towards a scientific career, both worked continuously in photography: he demanding of the image an "air of fact" and she concerned to capture and convey her subject's feelings. Even while Edwin worked as writer, editor and layout specialist for the FSA (1938–1943), both unofficially contributed records of their New England travels to the FSA file. Yet during this period, Edwin independently produced two documentary books, *Washington: Nerve Center* (1939) and *San Francisco: West Coast Metropolis* (1939), crediting his wife in the latter only for "all the dirty work, the developing of negs, the classifying, the note taking and some of the photography." She is acknowledged for having stayed "at my side at all times" and having "fought with me over ideas until, in her constructive opposition, they crystallized into workable projects." Not until Stryker's subsequent work with Standard Oil were they both again hired as equal and collaborative photographers. In 1946, the Rosskams left Standard Oil to begin an FSA-style document of Puerto Rico, and remained there until they returned to New Jersey (USA) in 1953. Edwin Rosskam died in 1984.

Marion Post Wolcott's interest in photography began with her studies at the University of Vienna during the early 1930's. But it was her meeting with Ralph Steiner of the Photo League in 1936 which prompted her seriousness, and encouraged her to freelance for the Associated Press and *Fortune* before getting her first staff job with the *Philadelphia Evening Bulletin* in 1937. In 1938, she was given a rare full-time appointment with the FSA, at a time when Lange had been refused one, and the only other two full-timers were Russell Lee and Arthur Rothstein. Although her work by no means conformed to her assigned brief, she was asked primarily to record the progress already made by the FSA. During the war her husband's travels took her away from her photographic practise. But she has recently begun and exhibited a new body of colour work.

Dorothea Lange is perhaps the best known of all FSA photographers, her image of the "Migrant Mother" now virtually an icon of the period as a whole. After formal studies with Clarence White at Columbia University, and her early practise as a portrait photographer in San Francisco, her interest turned emphatically to a more socially conscious practise. In 1935, she began her first records of migrant farmworkers, working jointly with her husband and sociologist, Paul Taylor, for the Division of Rural Rehabilitation of the California Relief Administration. On the strength of that early report, urgent sanitary camps for migrants were funded, and both Lange and Taylor were transferred to Stryker's agency in Washington DC. In addition to the many images which circulated widely alongside reforming articles in newspapers and journals nationwide, she and Taylor produced the documentary book *An American Exodus* in 1939, based on the quoted observations of their subjects. After her FSA work, she continued making documentary images, including many for *Life*, until her death in 1965. A retrospective of her work was mounted by the Museum of Modern Art in 1966.

Additional biographical information on Esther Bubley, Martha McMillan Roberts and Louise Rosskam can be found in S. W. Plattner, *Roy Stryker: U.S.A., 1943–1950*, Austin Texas, University of Texas Press, 1983. On Dorothea Lange and Marion Post Wolcott, see extensive references in P. Dixon, *Photographers of the Farm Security Administration, An Annotated Bibliography: 1930–1980*. For Marion Post Wolcott see S. Stein, *Marion Post Wolcott: FSA Photographer*, Carmel California, Friends of Photography, 1983, pp. 44–48.

The Photographs

Dorothea Lange. Migratory family traveling across the desert, U.S. Highway 70, in search of work in the cotton. Roswell, New Mexico. May 1937.

14

Dorothea Lange. A mother in California who, with her husband and two children will be returned to Oklahoma by the relief administration. This family has lost a two year old baby during the winter as a result of exposure.

Dorothea Lange. Desert Highway 70, the route on which many refugees cross. New Mexico. June 1938.

Dorothea Lange. Billboard on U.S. Highway 99 in California, part of a national advertising campaign sponsored by the National Association of Manufacturers. March 1937.

Dorothea Lange. Mexican truck driver's family. Imperial Valley, California. June 1935.

Dorothea Lange. Farm Security Administration mobile camp for migratory farm labor. Baby from Mississippi left in a truck in a camp. Merrill, Klamath County, Oregon. October 1939.

Dorothea Lange. Entrance to Amalgamated Sugar Company factory at the opening of the second best season. Nyssa, Oregon. October 1939.

Dorothea Lange. Mexican migrant woman harvesting tomatoes. Santa Clara Valley, California. November 1938.

Dorothea Lange. Native of Indiana in a migratory labor contractor's camp. "It's root, hog, or die for us folks." Calipatria (vicinity), California. February 1937.

Dorothea Lange. Tenant farmers displaced by power farming. Farmer, Texas. May 1937.

Dorothea Lange. Tenant farmers who have been displaced from their land by tractor farming. Texas.

Dorothea Lange. Mexican field laborers, on strike in the cotton picking season, applying to FSA for relief. Bakersfield, California. November 1938.

Dorothea Lange. Mexican woman at the US Immigration station. El Paso, Texas. June 1938.

Dorothea Lange. Destitute pea pickers in California, a 32 year old mother of seven children. February 1936.

Dorothea Lange. Dustbowl farm, Coldwater district. This house is occupied; most of the houses in this district have been abandoned. Dalhart (vicinity), Texas. June 1938.

28

Marion Post Wolcott. Buildings on main street of a ghost town. Judith Basin, Montana. September 1941.

Marion Post Wolcott. Building on main street of a ghost town. Judith Basin, Montana. September 1941.

Marion Post Wolcott. A farm. Bucks County, Pennsylvania. June 1939.

Marion Post Wolcott. Coal mining community. Welch, West Virginia.

Louise Rosskam. Control room at the water works on Conduit Road. Washington DC. September 1940.

Marion Post Wolcott. Corn shocks in a field. Frederick (vicinity), Maryland. February 1940.

Marion Post Wolcott. A barn on rich farmland. Bucks County, Pennsylvania. June 1939.

Dorothea Lange. Corner of the Dazey kitchen in the Homedale district. Vale-Owyhee irrigation project, Malheur County, Oregon. October 1939.

Marion Post Wolcott. Drug store window display in a mining town. Osage, on Scott's Run, West Virginia. September 1938.

Louise Rosskam. Proprietor of general store. Lincoln, Vermont.

Dorothea Lange. Men pause a moment to watch the Salvation Army, and then pass on. San Francisco, California. April 1939.

Dorothea Lange. Campaign posters in garage window, just before the primaries. Waco, Texas. June 1938.

Marion Post Wolcott. Negro man entering movie theater "colored" entrance. Belzoni, Missouri, in the Delta area. October 1939.

Marion Post Wolcott. A juke joint and bar in the vegetable section of the Glades area of south central Florida. February 1941.

Esther Bubley. Brother Edwin Foote preaching a sermon at the First Wesleyan Methodist Church. He wears sackcloth to reprimand the congregation for not attending a revival meeting held the preceding week. Washington DC.

Marion Post Wolcott. Movie advertisement on the side of a building. Welch, West Virginia. September 1938.

Marion Post Wolcott. Center of town. Woodstock, Vermont. March 1940.

Marion Post Wolcott. Young people in a "juke joint" and bar in the vegetable section of the Glades area of south central Florida.

Louise Rosskam. Old Edison victrola in a farm house. Bristol (vicinity), Vermont. July 1940.

Marion Post Wolcott. Miner who has worked in the mine since he was 14 years old and has tried to save money and have a better home, with his wife who suffers from a bronchial condition and asthma. Chaplin, on Scott's Run, West Virginia. September 1938.

Marion Post Wolcott. A more prosperous miner listening to the radio when he returns home after working on a night shift. He is Polish—his wife Hungarian. These "foreigners" are generally thrifty and their houses are cleaner than most. Westover, Scott's Run, West Virginia.

Marion Post Wolcott. Children in the bedroom of their home. Their mother has tuberculosis, their father works on WPA. Charleston, West Virginia. September 1938.

Marion Post Wolcott. Coal mine tipple in foreground. Caples, West Virginia. September 1938.

Louise Rosskam. Air view of a cemetery and town. Lincoln, Vermont. July 1940.

Marion Post Wolcott. Road, wheat and corn fields. Harvre (vicinity), Montana. August 1941.

Dorothea Lange. San Francisco, California, seen from the First Street ramp of the San Francisco-Oakland Bay bridge.

Marjory Collins. Shopping district just before closing time at 9 pm on Thursday night. Baltimore, Maryland. April 1943.

Esther Bubley. The wailing room at the Greyhound bus terminal. Pittsburgh, Pennsylvania. September 1943.

Esther Bubley. Children playing in a fountain in Dupont circle. Washington DC. July 1943.

Esther Bubley. Soldiers looking at the statue in front of the Federal Trade Commission building. Washington DC. March 1943.

Esther Bubley. Washington DC.

Esther Bubley. Soldier in front of Capitol Theatre. Washington DC. 1943.

60

Esther Bubley. Boarders often speculate on the identity of the owner of the house across the street. They like to think it belongs to the president of a South American steamship line. Washington DC. January 1943.

Esther Bubley. 1943.

62

Marjory Collins. Mrs Frank Romano putting her baby to bed. Her husband works in the Brooklyn navy yard. New York, New York.

Esther Bubley. Sally Dessez, a student at Woodrow Wilson High School, in her room. Washington DC. October 1943.

64

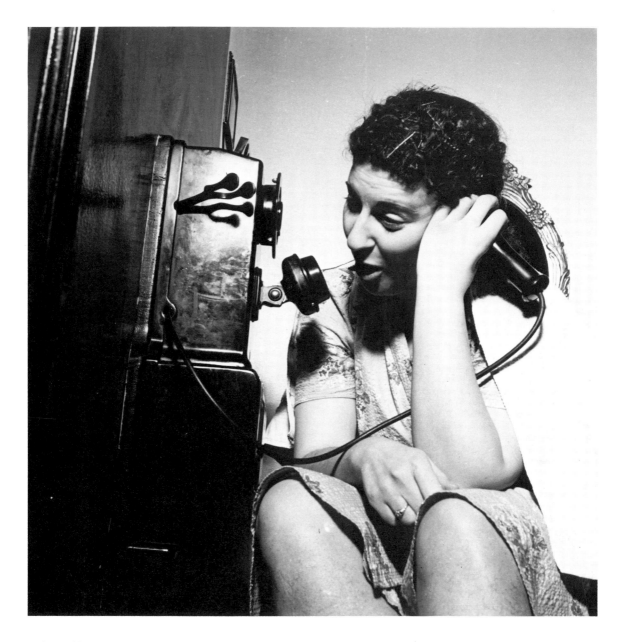

Esther Bubley. The telephone in a boarding house is always busy. Washington DC.

Esther Bubley. Women gossiping in a drugstore over Cokes. Washington DC. 1943.

Ann Rosener. National Exhibition at the Library of Congress of paintings, photographs and posters dealing with aspects of war, made by high school students from all over the country. A boy with one of the cut-outs. Washington DC. June 1943.

Marjory Collins. Armistice day parade. Lancaster, Pennsylvania. 1942.

68

Marjory Collins. Window of a Jewish religious shop on Broom Street. New York City, New York.

Esther Bubley. In the lounge at the United Nations service center. Washington DC. December 1943.

Marjory Collins. Photographer's display on Bleecker Street. New York, New York. December 1942.

Esther Bubley. In a hall of a boarding house. Washington DC. January 1943.

Ann Rosener. Blood donors enjoying light refreshments before leaving the American Red Cross Center. Washington DC. June 1943.

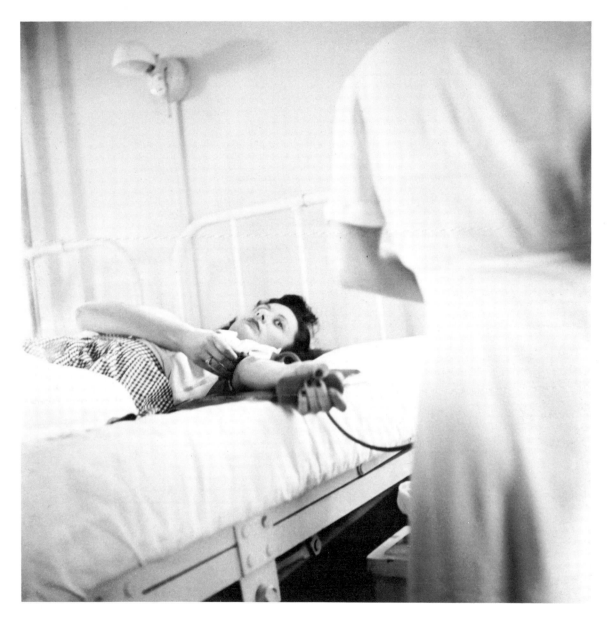

Ann Rosener. Blood donor at the American Red Cross Blood Bank. Washington DC. June 1943.

Marjory Collins. Third Avenue and 42nd Street from the steps leading to the elevated train. New York, New York. 1942.

Marjory Collins. St Mark's Place and the Bowery at midnight. New York, New York. September 1942.

Marjory Collins. Turkish night club on Allen Street. Guests get up and dance to the oriental music whenever they please. New York, New York. December 1942.

Marjory Collins. Sunday School picnic on the edge of the Patuxent river, given by Reverend Mr Jenkins of All Faith Church, and Mr Dale, local plumber and electrician, who teaches Sunday School. The church is attended by citizens of Mechanicsville and Charlotte Hall. Some watched while others waded in, the water was too shallow for swimming. St Mary's County, Maryland. July 4 1942.

Marjory Collins. Recently employed women being sworn into the Rubber Workers Union at a Sunday meeting. Most of them have never worked before and know little about trade unionism. Buffalo, New York. May 1945.

Louise Rosskam. Victory gardening in the northwest section. Washington DC. May 1943.

Ann Rosener. OWI research workers. Washington DC. May 1943.

Ann Rosener. Italian-Americans at work on a bomber in the Douglas aircraft plant. Santa Monica, California. February 1943.

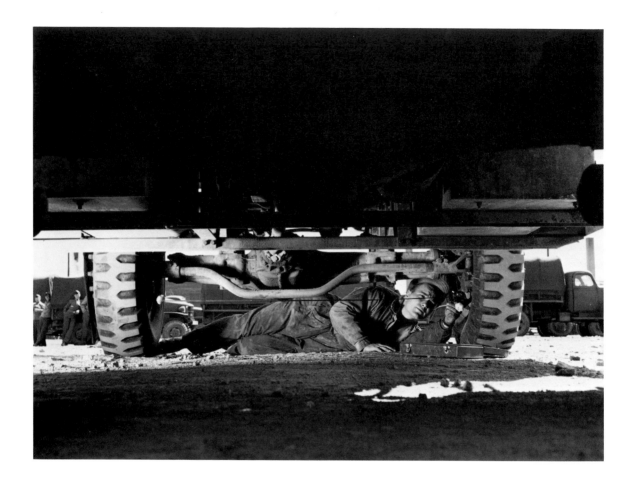

Ann Rosener. Periodic complete vehicle inspection is required of all US army drivers. This soldier is checking the wheel alignment of his truck, an important factor in the length of life of tyres. Holabird ordnance depot, Baltimore, Maryland. May 1943.

Pauline Ehrlich. Detail of a hay baler showing rotating knives which cut hay into proper lengths. Dresher, Pennsylvania. July 1944.

Martha McMillan Roberts. A torpedo plant worker and her family from Ohio, living in a trailer camp. Alexandria (vicinity). March 1941.

Pauline Ehrlich. Detail of baling machine showing hay being picked up at the Spring Run farm. Dresher, Pennsylvania. July 1944.

Ann Rosener. Permanente Metals Corporation, Shipbuilding division, Yard no. 2. A. Renati has worked in the yard for one year, and was formerly a florist. He was born in San Francisco, but both parents were born in Italy. Richmond, California. February 1943.

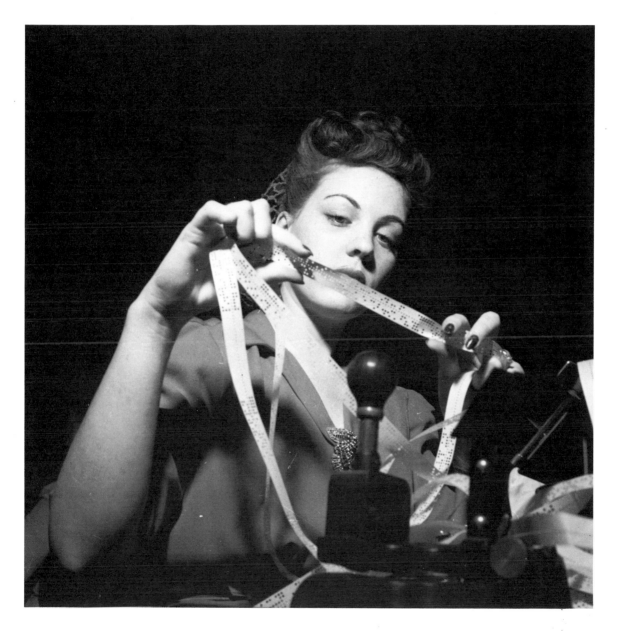

Esther Bubley. Miss Genie Lee Neal reading a perforated tape at the Western Union telegraph office. Washington DC. June 1943.

Martha McMillian Roberts. Three sisters at the cherry blossom festival.

Esther Bubley. Little boy riding on a streetcar. Washington DC. April 1943.

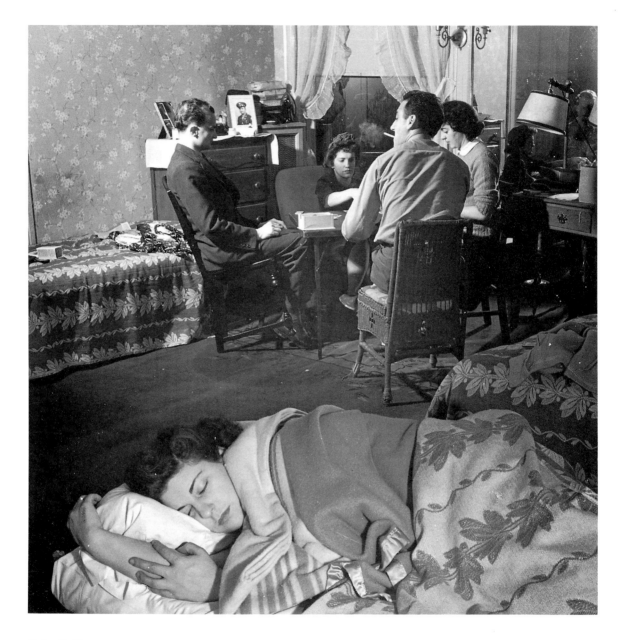

Esther Bubley. 1943.

Esther Bubley. Students at Woodrow Wilson High School. Washington DC. October 1943.

92

Esther Bubley. Washington DC. 1943.

Marjory Collins. Sleeping in a car on Sunday in Rock Creek park. Washington DC. June–July 1942.

Esther Bubley. Girls in the cafeteria flock around a sailor who graduated in June and is spending part of his french leave visiting Woodrow Wilson High School. Washington DC. October 1943.

Esther Bubley. Girl sitting alone in the Sea Grill, a bar and restaurant waiting for a pickup. "I come in here pretty often, sometimes alone, mostly with another girl, we drink beer, and talk, and of course we keep our eyes open. You'd be surprised at how often nice, lonesome soldiers ask Sue, the waitress to introduce them to us." Washington DC. April 1943.

Writing Memory

Intensities in the Present

☐ Over 200,000 photographs, taken for the Farm Security Administration and the Office of War Information between 1935 and 1943, are stored in the Library of Congress, Washington DC. With their location in that august architectural space is constructed our "discovery" of a past. The library itself seeks to establish our identity in the present by a play of distinction from the past. But the incursion of these documents of the past *into* our present designates its locus a play in difference: within it, history unfolds as the difference of times. Across our encounters with these remains of different moments, we locate ourselves as the dispersion of many selves.

We have no access to the past, but only to its residues in these documents. And these cannot function as ciphers for the recovery of our forgotten origins. They exist not as phantasms of the repressed, but as material things whose ordering comprises the archive. As objects in the present, they incite difference as the process of the present. The present is not linear but a layering of moments: the shifts of our attention among remaining traces. Housed within the modern library, the photographs form part of that ceaseless drift. And across this drift, the self elaborates not as one but as inconsistent many.

As the focus of our fascination, the photographs refuse to be confined to a distant past. Through the intimacy of our involvement, their diverse meanings unfold. Our gaze continually returns to make sense of them again and again. And across our engagement with each different meaning, the images provoke a crisis in the intimate: the chimera of a stable identity gives way to our manifold selves.

As the writing of our many relations with the photographs, their history cannot simply recall a single forgotten tale. For their past becomes legible only in terms of our own incoherence. In the moment of their production, too, the stability of identity wavered. Throughout the 1930's and 40's, the fragility of the positions of "man" and "woman" was manifest in insistent efforts to fix the identity of the woman photographer. At varying times, she was pegged as a "mother," a "girl," or silently allowed to picture other women as seductively urbane. Yet even this seemingly simple sequence can now only be written with the words of the present. We have only the fractured terms—mother, girl, seductress—with which we now attempt to speak of the feminine. By engaging with documents remaining from the past, history thus elaborates the many masks of the feminine in the present. Yet the library attempts to curtail the past in its contemporary presence.

In architecture, the archive is a space of purity, tranquility, permanence. The monumental, milky marble corridors appear endless; their refusal of spacial demarcation obscuring our active passage; the energy of walking reduced to barely perceptible progress; the force and scale of the body relentlessly diminished. Our only anchors appear in monumental slabs of primary color, the giant double doors refusing any indication of what might lie beyond. Yet in their inviolate geometric perfection, even these remain ambiguous in scale: floating in the white like mathematician's diagrams in the ideal space of the untainted page. (Like impenetrable icons, framed at the distant ends of passageways, they are reminiscent, too, of post-war modernist paintings framed by the museum's austerity. They seem to self-consciously echo the monumentality, and the purity of form with which a Barnett Newman aspires to universal awe. And in connotation, they similarly set the library adrift between detached scientificity and universal humanism.)

Thousands of aging images of abject suffering are concealed within ordered rows of immaculate burgundy filing cabinets. The drawers roll smoothly open, and then click to close. Swivel armchairs on castors roll effortlessly over deep pile carpet. Highly polished surfaces on heavy pale wood tables further disperse the even source of light. Nothing interrupts; everything glides with the ease of the self-evident.

It is a space of technicist power. In its elaboration of technologies of knowledge—interlocking grids of information on film, disc, file—it becomes a preserve of professional expertise. The photographs become almost incidental to the machine, a mere support of the institution and its staff. It is the power of the expert over objects that insists, in which the objects themselves are interchangeable. Although officially open to the public, no one casually browses. To enter, one must affirm one professionalism with another, declaring an academic or curatorial project.

In the relation of the photographs to their context one is seemingly presented with a series of dichotomies: wealth *vs* poverty; impenetrable calm *vs* suffering and strife; expertise *vs* helplessness; cool scientificity *vs* incitements to compassion; urban sophistication *vs* the simplicity of country and small town. Across these apparent oppositions, the archive is set up precisely to create that distinction of past from present that will congratulate the present on its harmony. (Yet even harmony implies the peaceful play of social forces, and so opens the way for those forces to fall into conflict; but the library, as a technocracy, deals not in interaction but in the enumeration of atomized facts.) The library presents history as that which is divulged and returned to its concealment: a past sealed, and concealed, from the present.

In the safeguarding of "then" from "now" lies the seduction of the archive: the unfolding of a secret world as screen for fantasy. Like driving, the library affords the fantasy of motion, made safe by the assurance of place. Though a troubled world unfolds before us, we remain untouched. The organization of the file by social groups or social activity reduces the images to mere conduits of bygone fact.

We flick ceaselessly, restlessly from one image to the next, the stack of cards behind the one we have in hand pulling us forward: seducing us to narrativise, like flick books or even a movie. But the evenness of the story's tempo, its refusal to climax and resolve, only serves to increase our appetite. Instead of upsetting that expectation, it perversely heightens it. A world is opening before us, over which narrative mastery is constantly deferred. So we continue flicking, wearing the corner of the cards a bit further.

The archive "shelves" the 1930's as a period which was overcome, now neutered as part of the rich and varied legacy of a liberal and benevolent America: a caring nation, a nation of survivors. But the membrane that separates the archive from the city proves fragile. And the library's seclusion of "what was," paradoxically refers us to its obverse in "what is."

Outside, on the marble patio that removes the library from the chase of the city street, academics lunch and exchange reading lists for forthcoming university courses. But visitors from the street set up an almost stereotypic incursion. A ghetto box suddenly sounds and four black breakdancers have unfolded their worn corrugated card as dance floor in the middle of the patio. The academics divide visibly between those who ignore and those who enjoy.

The library is surrounded on two fronts by its refusals. It is constructed on two dichotomies: between itself and the 1930's, between itself and the incursion of street culture into the antiseptic center of town. How do these two relate to one another; and how are we to relate the unemployed of the 1930's to the unemployed of today? For, surely they are not identical, and there are no lessons which can be drawn *directly* from the workings of power then, to its workings today.

The breakdancers are not photographs. And they do not parallel documentary's placing of the poor as objects of benevolent power. The relation to power produced with their incursion cannot be subsumed in identity with the 1930's. The 1930's cannot be commandeered as model with which to understand a present crisis.

This writing does not attempt to make the 1930's visible, disinterring them from the dust of decades. In the archive, the photographs are neither dusty nor inaccessible, but sterilized in their visibility. It does not hope to make today visible by contradistinction with yesterday. Neither does it attempt to make today visible through its identity with yesterday. The relevance of the 1930's is not that we somehow make accessible today's poverty by showing poverty then; or even that we expose the power invested in documentary today by uncovering its workings then.

We cannot elucidate the exercise of power today through its exercise in the past. Rather the library becomes the locus of many parallel relations of power. It consists, at once, of the relations between users and professional staff, of the relation of viewers to the pictured poor of its documentary photographs, of the relations it incites between the present and the past it has "overcome" and the relation of the breakdancers to an institution of government. Yet each of these remains distinct: simultaneous though disparate moments in the present.

It is not a question of then *and* now, but of the then *in* the now. The library sets up the conditions in which we seek to position a "then" and a "now"—whether in sequence or in identity is only of secondary importance. Either way, its rhetoric is one of unities. And it makes inaudible the more provocative, tangential relations between modes of power which subsist inconsistently, within the present.

The Drift of Reverie

☐ Though I had come to the library in search of the work of women photographers, much of their work was, at first sight, barely visible.

The vast majority of images in the file were produced during the 1930's. These earlier images portrayed destitute families forced onto the road by dustbowls and depression, abandoned farms lost under drifts of sand, shanty towns by the roadside and migrant pickers in the fields. In the later 1930's, the focus of the documentary shifted into the small town and the marketplace, the prosperous farms and the landscapes they form. They are images which incite our integrity. Through them, we feel ourselves secure in either powerful benevolence towards the poor, or nostalgia for the myth of a cohesive past. In their invitation to stability, these are the images most amenable to the library's segregation of the past from an unperturbed present. Among them are the few popular images, and a wealth of little known material by Dorothea Lange and Marion Post Wolcott: the only women whose contributions to the file have previously been studied and exhibited.

But as I flicked through the photocards, the names of other women registered momentarily and receded as quickly. Another kind of image fleetingly appeared, but then slipped past, through my apparent blindness. Only later did I think about this process of passing over them, and return to pull out each of these "invisible" images to be seen in their provocative difference.

The works of Esther Bubley, Marjory Collins, Ann Rosener, Louise Rosskam, Martha McMillan Roberts and Pauline Ehrlich refuse to conform to expectation. Their subject matter, during the 1940's, had shifted into industry and civilian efforts to support the American involvement in the Second World War. But a more radical change penetrates these images in their approach to photography. Where the images of the 1930's seemed to confer on us the satisfaction of unity, these images arrest, unsettle, and provoke a sequence of disparate responses. The search for women photographers had led to the work of another moment, and another visual idiom.

The visibility of images in the file had been entirely contingent on my purpose there. Even with the dispassionate approach of an observer, it was not possible to peruse the whole of the past. For the work of the historian is always an act of making visible, and making a narrative from the objects thus called forth from the past.

The images from the 1940's overturn the relations of the library, and provoke the observer into an intimate enquiry. Through fascination, they provoke a loss of position, and absolve us of the constraints of a unified self. They open a flux of self: our elaboration of selves through the difference of partial truths.

Esther Bubley. 1943.

☐ A particular series of these images from the 1940's caught my eye. Something in their portrayal of men and women, immersed in melancholic reverie, seemed to seduce me, and then to overturn all familiar positions from which to accept them. Something of their overflowing, into spaces uncharted on a visual grid, cast suspicion on their promise of a visual presence.

Their fascinations turn on an offering of sexuality; so the overturning of position becomes instantly an intimate affair, lending these images their uneasy resonance. Instead of heightening erotic mystery, their subjects' removal unsettles our visual pleasure. Entranced rather than enlightened, it is not clear how we might set about handling them.

The images relate to one another closely; but through fascination, they refuse our overarching statements. We become deeply implicated in their reading: in the intensities they arouse in us. The very notion of a "reading" seems to loose its grip. There is no longer a photograph, an "object" on which we perform this creative process, but an indissoluble intimacy. There is no "object" to interpret, but neither is the photograph reduced to mere excuse for the unveiling of our pre-formed fantasies. In its specificity, it becomes the site of our emotional investment. And in that intermingling, we permit ourselves vulnerability and place identity on the line.

☐ In image after image, the body of woman becomes the site of an absence. Yet absence, as the opening on our desire for presence, makes her more precisely, the site of a promise immediately withdrawn. She becomes a snare, the seduction of presence, promptly deferred. Through the lure of a photograph's transparency, she *almost* appears, inciting an expectancy: in the "obviousness" of her existence as Other, she almost confirms our Self as discrete origin—almost summons that solid totality held out as the Subject's completion.

Yet, she stares away, with the oblique unfocussed gaze of her own fantasy. She sets in train a flow beyond the unified place of the Other. Ironically, the very body which promised position, ours no less than hers, provokes its inverse: an elaboration beyond One: an elsewhere in excess of the image, and thereby an excess invading the Subject's Imaginary. One is constantly sliding off the image, in imminent arrival forever postponed.

In remaining unpictured, her "elsewhere" insists as an enigma. "Elsewhere," across her multiplicity of spaces, integrity fragments. The body becomes dispersal beyond sight: the camera's evidence traversed by drift beyond knowledge.

Between image and its excess, she arrests us—disconcerted—on the very verge of the Subject's becoming. An eye/I is lured as authoritative vantage point from which each view appears as unques-

106

tionably true. With the fiction of her as stable One, arises the fiction of our knowing I/eye. But for all its pretense to command, this fiction unwittingly provokes its rivals; the I/eye entrains the history of its own troubled emergence, and repeatedly evokes its silenced predecessors. Through photographs of women's reverie, a fluidity is summoned, a heterogeneity repressed as the cost of unified presence.

Between the seduction of completion and the insistence of its failure erupts a nervous irritation: the edge of our own incoherence, and the collapse of Self as our most intimate imagining. Back and forth she carries us, across the fraught and endless narratives of fracture and self-composure. "What do I see in the image? Is it there, was it there, will it be there? Who is she, what is she doing, where is she? Is it me, is it her?"[1]

☐ As she sleeps, the arms, head, hair of a woman fall across the door of her open-top car. The image is highly sensuous; and we associate pleasure with security: with knowing a Self, however tenuous or fleeting, and its relation to the Other. Her absent body is replaced by a car: a classic disavowal of woman's lack and her re-presentation through a fetish. Horizontal strokes of light and shadow alternate

over her arm and onto the paralleling curves of her car. Through the extension of softly lit surfaces, it might be thought that face, arm and car become her one continuous skin.

A Self is thus empowered with the familiar fetishizing gaze—seemingly secure, as it circles unchanged through well-worn scenarios of desire/disavowal. It "knows" her, not through all the varied fictions she might incite, but as narcissistic mirror of its fears. It longs for her as confirming Other, but then—threatened by her difference—makes her one of the boys through her phallic car. In its obsessive circuit of self-preservation, a tyranny of fixed meaning threatens her.

We attempt this conventional reading: From the threatened fortress of the I/eye, the image is insistently co-opted as support. But defence proves a futile chimera, for the image continually escapes. Had she tilted her head to acknowledge our presence or met our gaze with hers, she might have conformed. But the closure of her eyes disturbs, and diverts us across the modulating surfaces of the image as a whole. Her presence emanates through unseen dreams, refusing to be known. The investment of an "I/eye" in the placing of a "her" is reluctantly superceded; and in its wake identity fragments; transforming in its mobility across proliferating parts.

The eye scans and shifts from the remnant of her arm to the intruding rump of another white bumper; from the rear view mirror she might have glanced in to the distant car it might have displayed. The rush for explanation falters. The attempt to construct the "real" narrative disintegrates before endless possible connections.

The I/eye darts around, unrealised as totality, engaging with and relinquishing a host of partial truths. It is "show(n) parts of bodies restituted to their wandering, to their libidinal intensity, and fragments of objects, surfaces, durations, depths, chromatic and tonal sequences, with which something like an orgasmic death can happen."[2] But through this death of the total I/eye, the image inaugurates new pleasures.

Where pleasure had promised a Unity, we find two distinct processes: though the fetishizing gaze attempts to seal her fate, the I/eye detours towards more fluid partial narratives. Without hierarchy, these two itineraries coextend: not the pleasurable "illusion" of unity "corrected" by a more complex "truth," but simply different alluring intrigues. At the point of a woman's ambivalent presence, two economies of pleasure intersect.

The image is wholly seductive. But where "seduction" aroused our hope for that momentary sweep of unconflicted feeling, the image is inconsistent. It is not one seduction but a play of many, repeatedly crossing and undermining one another. And it is her reverie, first and foremost, that creates the bridge for this crossing.

☐ Reverie doubles the absence of this woman: not only is her body obscured; her presence, too, eludes us through the closure of her eyes. And reverie doubles, no less, the *meaning* of her absence: For, where absence might have set our desire's scene, her own fantasy intrudes. Her absence might have freed the field to become our self-styled mirror, but it is her very *difference* from us that reverie underlines.

It has been argued that the Missing Woman forms a lynchpin in our social order; and the image can certainly be read as illustration of that point. But because this absence is one of reverie, it seems somehow to also set our order adrift.

The paradox of phallocentrism in all its manifestations is that it depends on the image of the castrated woman to give order and meaning to its world. An idea of woman stands as lynchpin to the system: it is her lack that produces the phallus as a symbolic presence .... Woman then stands in patriarchal culture as signifier for the male Other, bound by a symbolic order in which man can live out his fantasies and obsessions through linguistic command by imposing them on the silent image of woman still tied to her place as bearer of meaning, not maker of meaning.[3]

Asleep, the woman is seen without seeing. Without sight, she can envision no desires of her own.

She is the silent object with which we construct our own meanings and live out our own fantasies. Such is one reading that might convincingly be made; but it contains not only "her," but the image as a whole as mere reflex of a prior perfected order. It becomes but one more support of an unchanging system, so happily balanced as to leave nothing in excess.

But she is neither blind nor blindfolded; and sleep evokes that other sight of dreaming. Though she may become the target of desire, she is also immersed within desires of her own. While sleep may leave her powerless in the waking world, her silent desire also suggests a different register of power. Removed from sight's linear power of subject over object, dream encircles symbols with converging meanings. Seeing in this other intuitive relation, she resists incorporation and cannot be totally contained. Sightless through dreaming, she becomes not only object of a gaze but, at once, its obstacle.

In this simultaneity, she opens up a rift; but rather than declaring an embattled opposition, she meets the encroaching gaze with elusive strategies of digression. Her image does not supplant the phallic gaze with its "critique." She unveils no inner truth to supercede the seductive surface of masquerade. She is "... not one current, pushing and tugging, but different drives and tractions ... an aimless voyage, a collection of fragments impossible to unify ... its very drift giving the advantage of the strongest resonance now to one (...), now to another ...."[4]

Hers is not a refusal of the gaze, nor does she evade the vagaries of desire. Our readings of her presence cannot divide into the "either" "or" of positions in conflict, but elaborate into a complex multiplicity. Without her seduction, no hope would be aroused. And without that hope, no displacement of hope across endless partial fulfilments. In short, without our fascination, drift would not begin.

This movement, from order through its drift, is felt rippling across the image as a whole. It permeates its every element, creating at every sign oscillating options in meaning. The car is perhaps the most prominent case. With its status as stereotypical fetish, it invites the most familiar of voyeuristic readings. Yet, paradoxically, it becomes the very pivot for divergent directions of meaning.

With her placement in the car, disparate journeys are proposed: co-terminous, and condensed within that starting point. Envisaged differently in each, she swings in endless oscillation between power and its lack. A car implies travel, and the power of mobility: a power both hers, as she sits at the wheel, and relinquished as she drifts into sleep. Though she invites us to "hold" her in each definition, she endlessly slips: incomplete and incompletable.

With the car's steering wheel obscured and an empty seat beside her, we might assume her to be its passenger, driven by someone else. So it is perhaps to our surprise that we discover her at the wheel, in the place of potential command. (Yet, despite that "discovery" the former reading persists, tugging as undercurrent of the latter.) Were the car to move she would be, not passive adjunct but assured subject of its fantasized boundless desires. And, though the car remains immobile, and she in oblivious sleep, the wheel's evocation of travel makes her sleep into a journey of another kind. Her interior journey, or dream, takes on exactly the expansiveness of the car's windswept speed.

Sitting alone at the wheel she might have travelled in solitary pleasure. But the gaping absence besides her suggests she patiently awaits "his" return. The empty seat refocusses our reading of the dream: though her dreams appeared as unspoken bids for the aimless and unbounded, they are now curtailed to a precise and personalized longing.

As her positions multiply, so too the spaces that divide them. Between the driving and the dreaming, between our two readings of her dream, lies the dichotomy of feminine desire.

It is as though the fact of having a female point of view dominating the narrative produces an excess which precludes satisfaction. If the melodrama offers a fantasy escape for the identifying woman in the audience, the illusion is so strongly marked by real and familiar traps that the escape is closer to

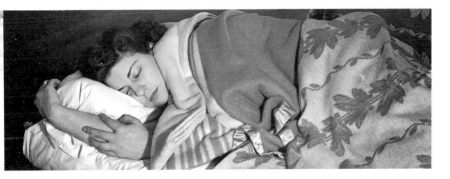

a daydream than a fairy story. (It) evoke(s) contradictions rather than reconciliation, with the alternative to mute surrender to society's overt pressures lying in defeat by its unconscious laws.[5]

The car may lend her dreams the mobility of travel, but they remain disappointingly as dreams. Her desire never reaches the convincing form of the fairy story, the illusory satisfaction of a photographed "real escape." Rather it remains an amorphous evocation as unconvincing and unrealizable as the daydream. And as in daydreams, her desires are always already counterscored by her visible immobility; she is *lost* in daydream, and precisely for that reason unable to realize dreams. As viewers we share in the fantasy of her eventual driven escape; but the illusion is marked from the beginning by the familiar trap of reverie's paralysis.

Hers is not a mute surrender to society's overt pressures, but an articulate evocation of its most painful contradictions. Her desire is neither suppressed nor denied, but emphatically referred to. The daydream is her power—beyond account, fluid and poetic in the layering of its meanings. But it nonetheless places desire in the form of its own spontaneous retraction. Whatever defeat she does suffer here is not the result of overt oppression, but of her own immersion within society's unconscious law.

Yet the contradictions persist, and her defeat is far from complete. In the face of familiar narratives in which the woman is overcome, the sensuous substance of her dreaming remains insistent. Moreover, the strength afforded her dreaming directs questions at our own implicit ranking of two countervailing pleasures. Against the linearity of driving, and the priority of "getting there," we have the poetic multiplicity, the "stationary drift"[6] of dream.

With her refusal of direction, she allows time the endless returns known only in reminiscence. "... female subjectivity as it gives itself up to intuition becomes a problem with respect to a certain conception of time ... time as departure, progression, arrival. It must also be added that this linear time is that of language considered as the enunciation of sentences (noun and verb; topic—comment; beginning—ending) and that this time rests on its own stumbling block, which is also the time of that enunciation—death. A psychologist would call this 'obsessional time' recognizing in the mastery of time the true structure of the slave. The hysteric (male or female) who suffers from reminiscences, would rather, recognize his or her self in the anterior temporal modalities: cyclical or monumental."[7]

By dreaming instead of driving, the woman abandons the linear hopes of departure and arrival. She abandons the constraint of desire into narratives that obsessively structure time: an "I" that wants a distant "it" and so drives over to "get" it. As metaphor for desire, the drive maintains a Subject and an Object; Departure and Arrival; a story with a Beginning and End. And like all such sequencing of time, the assurance that one will "arrive" and that desire sees a satisfying "end," immediately signifies its inverse. For the assurance of an end is also our terror. It is death which motivates the mastery of time, and death, paradoxically, which is evoked in that process.

In her dreaming such journeys are relinquished: for dream—like reminiscence—allows a circularity of time. It allows for the endless return of memory, the endless rehearsal of hopes, shifting slightly in their meanings with each appearance. She intimates another code for feminine desire, more akin to the poetic than to the structures of a story: a rhythmic ambiguity, a counter movement which destroys the logical simple finalities of language.

Our reading of the dream oscillates between power and its lack. Caught between these two terms, her desire remains ever in excess. It hovers at the edge, neither satisfied not completely quashed within the available positions.

☐ The car's implication of driving almost brackets our reading of the dream—almost contains it as a lesser form of drive. Likewise the car itself almost physically contains her body. But here again, disparate readings subsist, side by side. And as with the meaning of her dream, their ambiguity turns on the feminine position in desire: that is, her multiple positions, always exceeding the fixed scenarios of the voyeuristic gaze.

She is not only framed within the borders of the photograph, but re-framed within the boundaries of her car, she appears overwhelmed, and almost caged within the enormity of her vehicle. Against the deep shadow of the car's side and interiors, brilliant light picks out another "frame" across the hood, along the top of the doors, and across the folded car roof at the rear. This graphic device redoubles an already marked use of contrast, further darkening the interior as a cavern into which she disappears.

And beyond the containing order of her car, she is similarly placed within a wider visual grid. Repeated bars of stark reflected light pick out the fender in the foreground, top edges of her car, and the roof of the vehicle behind her, within this rigid structure, her space becomes a cubicle—a unit enclosed amongst identical others.

But her body's containment by the car goes far beyond its physical enclosure. For this is not just a relation of two objects, finite and stable in their separate significances. The car cannot be stripped of its

complex connotations to denote a means of transport, pure and simple. Neither is her body ever simply an obvious "woman-ness," a transcendent and immutable truth. Her placement in the car completely saturates our reading of her being; and likewise, her presence transforms our relation to the car.

As fetishistic disavowal/extension of her body, the car constructs a "look" and with it our relation to her as its object. Seen as fetish, and thus as stand in or extension of her body, the car's openness invites heightened scrutiny. Its openness becomes hers. She can become the locus of sexualized glamor, and through this openness, offer it up as accessible. Moreover, the car's open top carries the narrative of its opening. Like a curtain the roof has been retracted, implying a process of revelation or exposure. In this motion, she not only is literally displayed as we see her; more insiduously, *another* narrative is set in train of her own potential exposure.

But, paradoxically, it is equally this openness which pierces the seal of her containment. The very starkly lit edge which "framed" her also lays the basis for its breakage. For her head and arm fall across the container's perimeter; and a shadow falls onto the door, severing the continuum of the line which encircles her. The very openness that proferred her trap to our scrutiny proves to be her opening. She spills out, never wholly contained, over the very frame which delimited her space.

Had she been trapped before our investigative gaze, she might have been placed once and for all.

She might have been closed within the limits of an alluring lack, passive compliment to a phallic gaze. Yet somehow she exceeds this classification without needing to refuse it. Certainly, she draws us in on this familiar circuit of seduction; and she invites our power to scrutinize and define. But she overflows our definitions; she confronts the finality of our placing her with intimations of other positions.

The line of knowledge drawn around her immediately implies what exceeds it.

☐ And lastly, looking at the ease on her face, one wonders whether the trap has not in fact become, perversely, the source her comfort: not entrapment at all but envelopment. Though the car may read as entrapment of her body, it is equally another body softly enveloping hers. And in the sensuous fullness of that embrace are provoked memories of maternal plenitude. In the movement from entrapment to envelopment, we are absolved momentarily of longing and offered a fleeting but fond reminiscence. As the edge of her aloneness dissolves into her surroundings, the aim of the gaze obscures. Without its target, our desire dissipates giving way to the meanderings of fantasy.

Her envelopment consists not of the image content, but in the route of its visual seduction. It clearly

cannot arise directly from the banal occurrence of sleep at the wheel. Soft diffuse tones undulate across the image. The field accepts her into itself, gently shifting the eye from her across its other folds, dissolving the frozen boundaries of her separateness. With a quality of "presence" echoing assuringly throughout, she sleeps alone but not in isolation.

This function of the image as surface obstructs our reading of perspectival space. Met with this opaque grey veil, entreated into its sensuous textures, we have trouble in regaining our illusion of a photograph's receding reality. We have trouble both in fixing its place of origin, the I/eye behind the camera, and in locating the woman as object of that I/eye. Through this continual displacement of the gaze, we fix on the woman's body only accidentally, momentarily. The gaze consistently lets loose its focus—dispels the intensity of its own investigation—to elude the possibility of voyeurism.

When the image read as entrapment, we were lured to observe her. As Other, she incited both desire and the terror of her difference. At last she was held still before our investigatory gaze; and her car stood by as ready fetish when her threat of castration reached its heat. But when the image reads as envelopment, she bears the unfolding ambiance of plenitude. Between the fullness and the lack is entrained the history of the subject, the expulsion from maternal symbiosis into immutable separation, and desire without end. Through the intrusion of lack there emerges an "I," apart and able to address a

"You"; a subject both differentiated and differentiating, able to predicate and so immersed in the relations of language.

In the mother's absence, we retain only her image as object of our desires. Severance from absorbtion in maternal rhythm, tone and touch leaves only its trace in longing. At the point of loss, lingers only a specter: from all the unspeakable exchanges comprising the maternal space, there remains only the image as residue. But the image cannot revive or re-present all that has irrevocably been lost; such a web of simultaneous sensation, of its nature, resists this gathering up and pressing flat into the confines of a single sign. Instead of recapturing, memory replaces (represses) that boundless matrix with an "object." The emergent "I" finds a way to make known its demand for, at least, an acceptable substitute. From the stock of all that can, socially, be spoken or imagined, it pursues an arbitrary imposter. But capture of the imposter inevitably reveals its fraudulence—its paucity in relation to original loss; so it must continually be replaced by another, endlessly perpetuating an insatiable search.

Desire is thus marked by the primacy of the specular. The image takes hold as aim of its obsessive pursuits. And through its (deferred) promise of fulfilment it effects a forgetting of what went before: plenitude, as multiple and reciprocal registers of presence. When the car read as trap, and she its captured prey, her presence was utterly specular. It is not through reference to some fictitious "woman," but precisely as *image* that she becomes an "object" of desire.

But absorbed within her own enveloping plenitude, she refers us to that other scene, anterior to desire and to the primacy of the specular. She refers us to a scene which particularly persists for her as a woman. For her entry into language, and into the realm of desire holds a double dilemma for her.

Not only was the image interposed in the mother's place; but, upon entry into language, her longing is further submitted to the privilege of the phallus. Possessed by no one, it is revered as signifier of absence, par excellence. But while eluding both boy and girl alike, it nonetheless marks her different status. The phallus is defined as logically prior to the penis, in that it is the phallus which bestows significance on the penis. But a relation between the two is nonetheless posited. Through her repudiation as difference, they separate to address one another as speaking subjects.

For him, she becomes the locus of lack. But for the little girl, the fact that she has no means to represent lack results in her different relation to language. Her initial relation to her mother is "too full, too immediate, too present." She lacks lack, and so has little need of the images or words which stand in the place of absence: "... she has nothing to lose, nothing at stake.... Furthermore, in repeating, doubling the maternal body with her own the woman recovers the first stake of representation, and thus undermines the possibility of losing the object of desire since she has, instead become it."[8]

Enveloped within her car, the woman recalls this replete and fearless proximity. She allows herself the abandon of sleeping where public journeys converge; and amidst their imminent arrivals and departures, she emanates unruffled quietude. Hers is an intimacy unscarred by hesitation, or the weary imaginings of loss and violation; for her, longing extends not towards some "one," but around herself as sustaining aura.

☐ How ironic then that an *image* refers us to that plenitude; paradoxically it makes *visual* reference to that which precedes the rule of the specular. And on this ironic edge turns the possibility of engaging with envelopment in two quite different ways.

She may evoke an anterior to the image, but she cannot stand outside it. That tactile anterior must remain pure evocation, a reference rather than re-presentation. For having ruptured that plenitude, and entered the play of desire, there can be no direct return. Our every nostalgic attempt to draw nearer to that speechless "origin" must take the form of word and image. Moreover, the very notion of such an "origin" and the narrative unfolding from it, arise purely as retrospective fantasy. And perhaps our very belief in plenitude—whether early origin or wished for fulfilment—is merely the hopeful imagining of desire itself: not our past at all but mark of incompletion in the present.

Even envelopment, seeming obverse of the fetishist's entrapment, can be made to aggrandise the phallic gaze. Under the ubiquitous gaze, even memory of comfort can be lent a sinister violence. A woman's seeming completion may perversely provoke the fantasy of invasion. "The notions of integrity or closure in a text (or image) are like that of virginity in a body. They assume that if one does not respect the boundaries, one is 'breaking and entering', violating a property."[9] In its plenitude, the image incites precisely such invasion. Even envelopment, in the register of the specular can provoke such possessive violence.

The will to break in simply confirms the boundaries of the image. As discrete other, the image then confirms our autonomy. And the "erotic" implications of violation preserve the trajectory of desire: an I/eye potentially completed of the point of its arrival.

The law of desire co-opts all it sees. In its restless shifting amongst arbitrary objects, anything and anyone may equally become the idyll of its desperate, but ephemeral passion. Slipping, forever disappointed, from one object to the next, it attempts to press all into that uniform relation.

But this very strained attempt at totality implies the presence of that which obstructs: that perilous excess provoked by a feminine longing. Though the image may titillate with its taunt at violation, it refuses to stop there. And in the end we have still to deal with her envelopment as suggestion *beyond* the specular. We have still the enigma of that *other* pleasure, in the slippage of the eye from her as "object" into the enfolding tones of the image. Perhaps, however, her envelopment occurs not as "outside" of the specular, but as a special itinerary within it.

Diverted from its object into this aimless wandering, the I/eye dis-integrates from desire into fantasy. Bearings are lost, and it abandons that trajectory of desire which "positions and fixes the spectator as subject for its enunciation concerning a masculine Oedipal problem." Fantasy, by contrast, lays before the I/eye desire's *mise en scene* "... implying a splitting of the subject ... fantasy involves not an object of desire as in 'I' want 'x' but a scenario of activities which depend upon (...) participation ... The notion of the scene, a theatre; of role playing, ie interchangeability of roles."[10]

As the I/eye crosses and re-crosses the surface of the image it amorously engages with the spectacle of endless partial objects. It loiters momentarily, immersed in the seduction of each element in turn; but as quickly moves on to take up another invitation. And through this flight, desire's connection with any single object is never made.

Through this sequence of failed, but tantalizing identifications, the I/eye instead takes up each position interchangeably. It plays the role of each part in turn, relinquishing desire's attempt to complete a unified I/eye. In its movement it describes a scene in which each part unfolds into the others. Surfaces of metal and skin, glass and hair, ground and horizon meet in polymorphous intimacy, less through difference than through play. On the border of the specular, the journey of the I/eye describes an ambiance of multiplicity, of reciprocal exchange.

Through means of fantasy, the specular unwittingly lets loose its excess. Alongside the "pleasures" of breakage and entry, there persists this sensory envelopment. As intimate complement to our will to unity, there insists this most fecund unfolding of our desires.

Far from alternatives, these divergent regimes of pleasure consist in their interdependency—they arise and elaborate only in the course of their rivalry. And they are not just two, but an endless sequence of two's, piling up meanings upon one another like the readings of a dream.

☐ We seek her dream but in doing so create our own. Neither regime is ever established (for the image is wholly unbending towards the institution of order): so neither is the subject afforded (or confined to)

such stability. Like the fragment of a dream, we descend on the image as an opening on our own encoded passions. And like the dream's symbol, it becomes immediately the site of contrary desires.

She drives us right into the corruptions of the gaze. Her languid fall across the car unashamedly seduces. Yet it is only through this incitement to possess that we are also deflected off the visual frame. It is only through the imminence of her physical presence that we are lured into the image and then detoured on the route of her reverie. She remains inexhaustible; she is never possessed, and so never relieves (deprives) us of these dubious (indubitable) pleasures.

The pleasures of the image lie in our own unsettling.

☐ Fascination generates this endless sequence of slippages: slippages not only in the "issues" the pictures illuminate, but, first and foremost in the positions from which we look. The dichotomies opening through engagement with this one image are inflected again and again across others of the same moment. Seated beneath the sign, "Out for A Good Time," Esther Bubley's woman gazes away in vacant melancholy. Again, her literal accessibility is belied, or doubled, by another kind of presence. In its persuit, we are deflected off the image frame; yet our reading of her reverie remains informed by the sensuous diffusion

Ester Bubley. Listening to a murder mystery on the radio in a boarding house room. Washington DC. 1943

118

Ester Bubley. Washington DC.

of tone across the surface of the image. Like the woman in her car, she oscillates between power and its lack: her longing is held on the edge between dependent "longing for" and autonomous immersion in a capacity for dream. Both the kitsch candle of hope and the bald announcement of her sign lend a double edge to the narratives of a single woman's life: those hopes at once naively chased and ruefully disdained.

A dressing table top is cluttered with mementos of a woman who remains unseen. In their accumulation is evoked memory, longing, and in the clock's marking of time, narratives of loss. As a woman's own fetishes, they both describe and disavow the absence of those recorded there. There is obsessional love lavished in meditation on these dead icons; yet it immediately implicates intimacy itself as a site of absence. But she is not merely a site of loss, for these stand-ins for her desires equally describe a fullness: her extension into a space apart and a richness in her fragmentary passions.

Fascination provokes our presence as inexhaustible unfolding: progression towards a position of knowledge, perpetually deferred. Each image invokes its own fractures. In each, we pursue a maze of cross-contending narratives. Incited thus, in the place of a momentum, the I/eye arises as irredeemable becoming; identity is refused a location. Through simultaneous readings, we fabricate Self as multiplicity. In the ambivalence of each picture's pleasures, we relinquish the singularity of a moral summit. There is no vantage point from which the truth of the image will be revealed. The mirage of Self shimmers in the distance, and yet disintegrates on approach. Through coalescence and dispersal without end, fascination provokes us: not in the position of pedagogy but in the process of duplicity.

Our play of mastery falls away, and with it the classical relation of knowledge. The distinction of subject from object begins to blur; for how can we stand aside and hope to study that with which we are inextricably bound? And, most disturbing, our engagement intrudes on the relations of history: for fascination is always in the present, always ours. It is always profoundly amoral. For the contradictions "of the image" are immediately our fissures. The failure of the image to add up cannot be reduced to the expression of a problem in the conditions of its making, but must also immediately be ours.

Yet, despite this disavowal of the relations of history, history draws us with the urgency of memory. Like memory, it appears to be the crux of our identity; and like memory, it defies completion.

An Uncertain Exchange

☐ In August 1985, I went to New York to speak to Esther Bubley. And perhaps without knowing it, I was seeking to extend a kinship with her photographs to a kinship with their author.

Our conversation, however, became more interesting for its frictions than for its ease of rapport. In its faltering, it withheld the dream of an accessible flow of history. And at a disarmingly intimate level, it brought to light, and then brought into question, the profound expectations we invest in the stories of our pasts.

It was in no sense an interview, but rather an attempted exchange; for an interview would presume that the truth of these images, and the truth of their moment, could be spoken solely by their author. To conduct an interview, as conventional historian, would be simply to produce another document: an unassailable account whose veracity would underpin that of the documentary images themselves. To interview Esther Bubley would be to abdicate the unfolding of diverse fascinations in her images, before the authority of her final reading.

Perhaps, on the contrary, it was my attempt to confirm those most private fascinations through our mutual recognition. But through the difference of our perceptions of our intersecting pasts, our meeting proved at best sporadic. The images made quite a different sense to each of us. And out of this disjuncture arose the discomfort of each of us faced with our partial truths. Yet it was precisely this disparity that shed the most light on the production of her images and on the production of my writing. Like the images themselves, our meeting refused to confirm a unified position from which to recall one past.

Certainly, Bubley generously shared with me aspects of her professional background, and her perception of her work within the documentary projects of the Farm Security Administration and the Office of War Information. After a training in studio photography, and a temporary position with *Vogue* magazine, she had begun work with the FSA in 1941, not as a photographer but as a darkroom technician. Yet, she had gone out taking photographs in her own time as contributions to the file, and was soon promoted to become a staff photographer. She had been the last to follow in the footsteps of Arthur Rothstein and John Vachon, both of whom had worked their way up from the labs. Surprisingly, she had no contact with Ann Rosener or Marjory Collins, the other women concurrently employed as photographers, as they were "out in the field"; but she recalled several of the men who had remained close to Washington—John Vachon, Arthur Siegel, Ed Rosskam, Jack Delano and John Collier—with great respect. It was through them, and the documentary tradition which they upheld, that she developed her lasting commitment to documentary as opposed to art or fashion photography. Her photographs stood proudly in the tradition of Dorothea Lange and Walker Evans, whose works had already become the "classics" of the Farm Security Administration when Bubley started work with the agency.

During her three years with the FSA and OWI, she had seen the focus of documentary shift. Where the small town had earlier been repeatedly pictured as the paradigm for Americanness, the OWI emphasized the scale and efficiency of America's war industries and the impact of war on civilian life. What Bubley described as a "narrowing" was due, in her view, to Stryker's departure in 1941, and the loss of his personal visionary breadth.

Throughout, however, she felt that her own interests and abilities were slightly different from those of the men. Though working firmly within the documentary tradition, her feeling had been always for the more personal subjects. Where Walker Evans and John Vachon had shared Stryker's interest in the main streets, shop fronts and signs of the typical small town, she felt she had pictured them merely as an exercise. But, "put me down with people, and it's just overwhelming."

Without the detailed shooting scripts with which Stryker had directed others, she had set out after

Marjory Collins. R. H. Macy & Co. department store during the week before Christmas. New York, New York.

hours to locate *another* epitome of America. Through a sister who lived there she had been introduced to the boarding houses for single women, newly arrived in the city to work within the war effort. In their migration to the city, and in their hopeful visits to bars and dances on the army bases, these women were "looking for something": for men probably, but their restlessness seemed to her to touch on a more pervasive mood. It was in such personal sources of engagement that she seemed to have differed most. For she shared utterly in Stryker's commitment to straight unmanipulated photographs, in which Americans could speak honestly and simply for themselves. And like him, she believed that in its typicality, each image would transcend the individual to document a particular way of life. On a personal level, too, she fondly remembered the family-style gatherings of photographers for dinners in the Stryker home.

Yet it was over the significance of these events that she and I seemed not quite to meet. Where she disparaged the skills she had deployed at *Vogue* as irrelevant to documentary truth, they seemed to me to have played a pivotal role in the radical departure of her work from the "classics" of the 1930s. Where the frontality of the 1930's shot connoted a direct and immediate presence, her complex poses proposed circuitous routes in fantasy; and where the 1930's image had deployed flat lighting to signify natural and honest representation, her images were carefully inflected with evocative directional lighting.

Bubley thought very little of her lack of contact with Marjory Collins and Ann Rosener. Yet, in retrospect, it lends greater intrigue to the communality of their work. The move of both Bubley and Collins into urban subject matter seems to mark a new visibility and power of the city. And despite differences in their subject matter, both seem to have shared a concern with an urban play in artifice and with the transformations in sexuality emerging there.

Bubley's angelic blonde looks longingly towards the junk halo round an electric bulb. Collins ironically lends life to a female mannequin, peering down from her window display at her onlookers. Through a bizarre collision of junk culture and religion, the first invites seduction through a woman's ironic play in purity. The second presents woman as simulation itself. Both seem to knowingly remark on the place of the feminine as masquerade before an investigative gaze, yet both equally insist on identities other than that single mask. While inviting our pleasure at their display, they hint at that feminine identity as but one among many tenuous fictions. The gaze of Bubley's woman at her kitsch icon seems to pointedly parallel ours at her. Collins' woman returns the surveillance of those on the street. But while the feminine, in Bubley's and Collins' images may exceed the masquerade, that fiction nonetheless insists. Despite Collins' suggestion of her woman's repartee, a mannequin remains petrified as an object of display: the look of a doll remains an impotent response.

In their self-conscious sensuality, these women are far afield from the destitute migrant mothers of the 1930's. Yet, neither image is simply a transparent window on a changed urban woman. On the contrary, each is saturated in its very making with the artifice it describes. In both, the lighting carefully picks out the woman as object of our gaze. Not only are these women radically removed from the dustbowls and Depression, these photographs are far afield from the 1930's photographic conventions.

In a different context, and using different photographic strategies, Ann Rosener's work also marked a fundamental shift in sexualities. And like the work of both Bubley and Collins, her images do not simply document change; they are themselves made with both a self-consciousness and an ambivalence about emergent gender positions. Her images divide across the dichotomy in which women found themselves in wartime. On one hand, she pictured them in boilersuits, poised over heavy machinery and engrossed in the work of war industry. But on the other, they became almost parodies of classic feminine ideals: the doll-like girl in white chiffon gown, dancing spotlit in the arm of her model soldier, or the efficient modern mother enjoying her immaculate kitchen. In the bland perfection of each tableau, and across the divisions between them, Rosener, too, presents an unease with the placing of the feminine.

Though they worked quite independently, these three women now appear to have transformed documentary practise. The effect of immediacy which had lent the 1930's images their claim to social truth seems quite at odds with these women's subtle artifice. In the portraits of the 1930's, one was offered the fiction of confronting another person in the simple majesty of a shared humanity. One had the sense of knowing the other as an equal, and through that certainty also knowing oneself. To my eye, the images of Bubley, Collins and Rosener, on the contrary, unfold elusive and manifold meanings. And these shifts in meaning produce endless differences in the self we feel ourselves to be. Such differences in ourselves upset the relations of documentary truth: the perusal by a certain self over its known domain.

The "truth" of these images seemed to me to be of a different order: not of the integrity of each human being, but of our complexity. They spoke not only of a womanhood beyond them, but of the role of images and the process of looking in producing femininity. The images of the 1930's had used particular photographic conventions to construct the appearance of an untainted window of the world. But these images seem to take a pleasure in the artifice which is photography. And they use their articulacy with that artifice to set several notions of the feminine in counterpoint.

In this context of transformed photographic practise, the absence of contact among the three women becomes noteworthy; for it suggests that the changes were far more than individual. Each woman was quite separately dealing with a new range of tensions around gender and the image. Yet, in Esther Bubley's memory, she had simply recorded, with the compassion of the great documentarists, what had appeared to her typical of that historical moment. Though the world she faced in 1943 was inevitably different from that which Lange had known in 1936, the spirit of their work was, in her view, much the same.

From this difference in our perceptions emerged the exchange in which she and I were, perhaps, most out of step: surprisingly, it was over the source of her images' pleasure that we seemed farthest afield. I had still somehow expected that which so deeply engaged me to be shared by Bubley and others. In that instant of a photograph's seduction we remain blissfully unaware of our input in unravelling the pleasures of the image. And perhaps it is only the hesitations of a meeting like mine with Bubley that can arrest that seeming spontaneity.

In Bubley's view, the pleasure, or value, of her work lay in the compassionate recording of objective social truth. She had set out with the 1930's hope for the photograph as potential lever towards necessary social reform. The photograph was, for her, an instrument of purpose and of understanding.

Amidst her foregrounding of documentary claims, the ambivalent longings emerging for me in her work seemed almost unspeakable. In the intimate spaces established through pose and lighting, I felt her very different kind of photograph excited sensuous intensities unseen in the earlier documentary work. But, from her point of view, any aberration from the procedures of the thirties would have diverted her work from her central concerns. So when I asked about the posing and lighting I came perilously close to that suggestion. Yes, she had taken photofloods onto her locations: it seemed a reluctant statement, but only because she appeared to think it an insignificant detail.

Though visible, the very kernels of my fascination remained inaudible. And though each of us invested the passion of her being in these images, token intermediaries in our contact, our intimacy had simply never begun.

Esther Bubley. 1943.

126

☐ Our conversation allowed no access to continuity. It refused the view of the past as purposeful unfolding of our common essence; and so refused to grant the fantasy of one essence. There was no enduring common identity: no fullness with which to assuage the fractures of the present.

We are endlessly embroiled in attempts to narrativize our pasts—through memory, dream and the production of legitimized histories. In casting that retrospective line behind us, we pinpoint our present location. And in the extension of the line before us, we gather the momentum of seeming progress. At its furthest point, on the far horizon, we project our fantasy of completion.

In the hope for a kinship between myself, as woman spectator, and the woman photographer whose images I enjoyed, perhaps such a fantasy of completion had been at play. In that primordial mirroring we might have imagined the identity of "woman" as continuous and enveloping. But Imaginary it is, for it would offer women the Utopian promise of a full, unchanging communality and from it an alternative language in which the feminine spoke uninterrupted. (Mis)recognition of gender as whole would find its mirror in a unified self-image.

To search through this history for an image of "woman" once more makes her the object of a look. Already, woman is massively defined, confined, examined. The weight of "difference" falls upon her. In the dual positioning of "masculine" and "feminine," she alone is seen. Her body becomes the prime site/sight at which the sexual emerges as visible. She is that site of spectacular fascination where the energies of sexuality traverse. Sexuality is defined not by her, but in the gaze at her image. To seek, across these images, a unified Woman's Eye, would be to simply reproduce the relations of her silence.

In my talk with Esther Bubley, there was no lost origin round which the fractures of the present might coalesce. She had not confirmed my sensibility by conferring on it a continuum; nor had she recounted a moment from which to trace the myth of my becoming. Rather, we faced in each other, the persistence of differing partial truths within the present.

We were not divided as mere representatives of atomized historical moments: she was not the voice of a distant past, nor I the voice of a subsequent progress. Each spoke in the present across a gap which is itself the present. Though our liaison lacked ease, its result was far from resignation before unbridgeable ruptures in time. Neither the history of continuity, nor a history of rupture could make sense of this encounter of partial truths. For even a history of rupture, of continuity refused, requires a writer who "knows." From a privileged position of vision, a coherent writing proceeds. Though its historical moments may be absolute in their distinction, the text which describes them remains a seamless whole. Though perhaps robbed of a linear progression, the dream of coherence remains inviolate.

Yet the photographs that fascinate, those to which we inescapably return, speak eloquently not of unities but of the fragility of our presence. We cannot speak of them from one position because they, themselves, provoke our multiplicity. And they make possible the production of that multiplicity across disparate forms of writing: a simultaneity of relations to the material. Each balances on the other so that none claims the primacy of truth. Each opens on another so that no collection, however diverse or extensive, can exhaust the total account.

Between a coherent history and a history of rupture may lie another address to the past: a writing shot through with desire, and which may remain as fragmentary and devoid of destination as desire itself. In writing, the subject permits the wandering of each fragment off centre, dispersing across the present's inconsistencies.

Perhaps it is yet possible to have a curiosity about these women photographers, even a sense of kinship, which does not submerge us in longings for identity. Perhaps there is an engagement with this

Ann Rosener. All nursing and no play might make Frances Bullock (right) a dull girl! To preclude such a possibility Army nurses hold dances in the nurses' home.

Ann Rosener. Saving waste fats and greases from which war materials will be made. Washington DC. September 1943.

history which does not close down to gender fixity; but which, on the other hand, does not erase itself in the endless specificity of moments, eradicating any resonance from one to the other.

In my meeting with Esther Bubley it was not our unified speech but the interstices between us which sounded loudest. So perhaps attention might turn from the disappointments of unity to the intrigue of the gap: the mark of difference that sets the present in process.

Across disparate approaches to writing, fragments of ourselves are provoked and set adrift. The writing of the subject's dispersal in relation to the image of a woman asleep in her car, the memory of meeting a photographer, and an attempted "historical" narrative (which follows) may all float, side by side, as partial evocations of a related past.

Each writing calls forth its own materials from the residues comprising the archive. Each writing directs our present day attention through its own circuit of remains. In their inter-relation, such writings construct history as a play of difference in the present. Such a history "establishes that we are difference ... our history the difference of times, ourselves the difference of masks." Far from being the complete account of something that lies behind us, it is the making present of the "dispersion that we are."[11]

A Crisis in the Intimate

☐ For varying periods between 1935 and 1943, Dorothea Lange, Marion Post Wolcott, Louise Rosskam, Martha McMillan Roberts, Marjory Collins, Pauline Ehrlich, Ann Rosener and Esther Bubley took photographs for the American government.[12] Amongst these, only the work by Lange and Post Wolcott has been exhibited, studied, and reproduced.[13] Yet the history of women's relations with documentary is far from one of simple exclusion.

Throughout this period, women were employed to take photographs though they were taking photographs from positions different from the men photographers. But the distinction of their position is not one of discrimination. They are not simply an occasional presence, employed as an excuse for a liberal tokenism. They were neither relegated to trivial or marginal roles, nor hidden from visibility.

Revelation hardly seems necessary in a context where Lange, at least, is widely hailed as a heroine of her moment, and Post Wolcott's work has recently received increasing attention. And what emerges within the massive visibility of these two is how little their positions had in common. On the contrary, it seems that the *difference* in women's positions was renegotiated at each juncture. At each point, the difference in their positions had quite distinct implications for both their access to the profession and the prevalent readings of their work. Moreover, at each juncture, the position of the women photographers proved crucial in constructing shifting notions of documentary truth.

During the "classic" period of FSA photography, from 1935 to 1937, Dorothea Lange became a key figure in securing the humanism of documentary. She was repeatedly represented in popular journals as the "mother" of documentary: the little woman who would cut through ideas by evoking personal feeling. Through her pathos for destitute rural migrants, the New Deal's programs of rural reform might be legitimized, not as power, but as the exercise of care. Her place in the construction of documentary rhetoric was thus crucially different but every bit as important as Walker Evans', more widely recognized as the paradigmatic figure of documentary. Where Evans was thought of as the guarantor of honest observation, with his flat-lit frontal shots, Lange was lauded as the keeper of documentary's compassion.

Marion Post Wolcott, hired by the FSA in 1938, played a crucial role in negotiating a shift in the project and in the pictorial rhetoric of documentary. The political coalition that had sustained New Deal reform was beginning to strain; with the onset of the renewed "Roosevelt Depression" in 1937, its defectors increasingly questioned its efficacy. Post Wolcott was given a full-time post in preference to Lange, precisely because she was charged with inaugurating a very new work. As a woman, her brief was to assuage, with positive records of the FSA's rural resettlements and of American life in general, particularly through eulogies to the small town and the land.

The period from 1940 to 1943 was marked by wartime mobilization, and returning economic prosperity. In the final period of documentary work done by the FSA and the Office of War Information, Stryker took on a whole number of women photographers: Martha McMillan Roberts, Marjory Collins, Esther Bubley, Pauline Ehrlich, Louise Rosskam and Ann Rosener. It was at this point that women photographers gained most free access to the profession, but by this point the demands of the agency had changed substantially. They were hired to produce propaganda as versus documentation, recording war work and the effects of war on civilian life. With attention turned to the war, little was spoken of the women photographers and their work was rarely by-lined. Yet women are insistently present in their photographs as the locus of emergent desires: newly arrived in the city to work within the war effort, dislocated and presented as sites of longing. Geographically, the women photographers worked mainly in the city, safe from an "unladylike" outback. As documentary became potentially a woman's work, it also became a very different work.

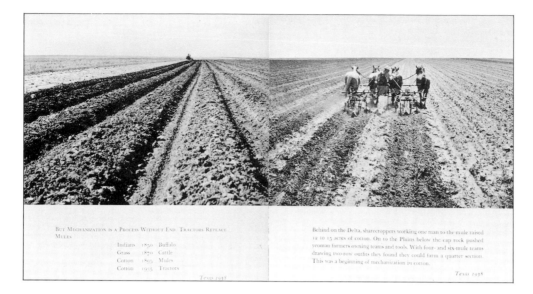

Dorothea Lange and Paul Schuster Taylor, *An American Exodus: A Record of Human Erosion*,
Reynal & Hitchcock, New York, 1939, pp. 70–1.

Far from becoming the invisible victim of discrimination, the woman photographer was prominently presented, initially as the mother and then as the charming girl who would ease the strain of social conflict. And though a silence surrounded the figure of the woman photographer in later years, that silence is not indicative of her continuous refusal but of the conditions confronting her in one particular moment.

Through vociferous public discourse, the woman photographer was positioned as mother, as charmer, and latterly as invisible. But in their incessant repetition, these statements appear not as descriptions of roles wholly inhabited, but as attempts to fix positions which continually slipped away. They describe not positions held, but bids for position tendered amidst a confusion surrounding the difference of the woman photographer.

The flux in power provoked by the 1930's social crisis was, at once, a flux in positions of personal identity. The collapse in consensus about the nature of society was, at once, a crisis in the intimate: a collapse in consensus about the identities of men and women. Countervailing claims on social power unfolded through a contest to define the nature of the crisis and thus the direction towards its cure. And with this social power would come the prerogative to name the positions in personal identity which lie within it.

The naming of the woman photographers was thus implicated in pervasive tensions surrounding positions of gender. And in its prominence, it took a crucial part in attempting to secure definitions of the feminine.

Through its claim to represent reality, documentary photography was at the centre of the flux in social power. And as participants in the production of these photographic truths, women, too, attempted to settle the uncertainties of social crisis. The relation of women to truth became equally their relation to power. For the prerogative to establish a truth was, at once, a status of power.

Yet, the uncertainty surrounding power was only redoubled by the uncertainty surrounding the nature of women. So, rather than securing women's power, the relation of "woman" to "power" only served to interrogate both terms.

The photographs change dramatically across the period, yet each in its moment became credible as transparent window on the world. From the mid-1930's to the mid-1940's, it was not just the pictured world which changed, but an entire approach to the making of pictures. It was not simply that the world had transformed from one of sacrificial mothers and hardbitten fathers in the 1930's to one of wholesome soldiers and moony office girls in the 1940's.

The locus of truth which had been gathered around one type of image disintegrated, and reformed around another and another. Where, in the mid-1930's, it had been flat lit frontal simplicity which guaranteed an untainted truth, by the mid-1940's it was self-conscious composition and languid pose. In the 1930's, the image emphatically fell away to reveal an agrarian expanse beyond; but in the 1940's one is held ambiguously between allusion to the "real" of a city space, and an opaque undulation of image surface. The image itself partakes in the city's self-conscious play in artifice.

In the face of such marked transformations in style, exclusive claims to truth made by one idiom are thrown into question. Though each documentary style argued the supposed "scientificity" of its camera, each returned with quite different results. The camera, as mechanical instrument, provided no assurance of a neutral and therefore consistent, image.

The truth effect of documentary rests with a rhetoric woven around the image, continually traversing both its production and its reading. It was not the photographs alone which convinced the urban populace of a crisis calling for action in the countryside. They might equally have been understood as artistic expressions of inner vision, as they were soon afterwards.[14] Their truth-effect consisted in the complex intersection of the image with both pervasive claims for the honesty of the instrument and the social reforming arguments which accompanied them in newspapers, journals and exhibitions.

The meaning of the image thus became inseparable from these converging rhetorics. And the prerogative to persuade with such a rhetoric lies with power. Only with power may rhetoric be convincingly presented, not as persuasion, but as objective report.

Richard Wright, *12 Million Black Voices: a folk history of the Negro in the United States*, Viking, New York, 1941, pp. 50–1. *Photographs by Dorothea Lange.*

We plow and plant cotton

Our lives are walled with cotton

The Depression was a crisis in an entire regime of truth. As such, it was also a crisis in authority. Newspapers, radio and government officials, the established mediators of social information, had systematically downplayed or ignored the extent of the crisis. In the wake of the 1929 crash, mass unemployment and evictions in the city, and drought, foreclosures and destitute migrations in the countryside were met with only minor monetary reforms from President Hoover. There was neither relief provided for the unemployed, sick or homeless, nor protection for their rights to organize.

The press was no longer believed by the people; it had fallen out of step with its audience. The crucial event in this repudiation was the 1936 election. More than 80% of the press opposed Roosevelt, yet he won by the highest percentage ever. And that repudiation was not just passive cynism, but an actively expressed hostility. When Roosevelt motored through Chicago after his election the crowd was cheering not only in support of him, but jeering and shouting slogans against the press. In electing him, they clearly felt that what had been defeated was not only his opponent, but an entire informational network.[15]

Irreparable rifts had opened between people's desperate experience and fragmentary word-of-mouth knowledge of the crisis, and the anodyne view offered by those in whom they had invested their trust. The collapse in their credibility was, as a result, not simply a demand for better information from the

existing authorities. Acquiescence in having "reality" mediated by those on high erupted into a call to have reality speak for itself. The established "reality" had been predigested for the common man as its silent and invisible object. A democratization was now demanded through the representation of the common man, by the common man.

It was in response to this pressing demand that the rhetoric of documentary emerged. It became a rhetoric in which the photograph, as re-presentation, was elided in the hope that its subjects could speak for themselves unimpeded. Claims of particular types of image to achieve this transparency were vehemently debated in a wide range of popular journals, symposia, radio discussions, and social and political groups.

Far from its present seclusion within a "profession," the rhetoric of documentary was an insistent and pervasive speech. It was a speech impelled by a crisis in power, and one which was consequently invested with multiple attempts to supplant that power. Everywhere, the nature of reality, and therefore the means of its transformation were open to contest.

Within the workers' photography movement the crisis was construed within the terms of class oppression and revolutionary change. Masses of demonstrators from cities all over the country were montaged together to visually comprise a combative class. Where the individual appeared at all, it was as heroic helm of that monolithic army. In early FSA photography, by contrast, the problem was constructed as natural. The wrath of nature had been visited upon helpless though virtuous victims. Its solution was sought through liberal reform, in which the government retained exclusive power over the salvation of private farmers. Visually, the victims remained atomized in their suffering: the focus of a comfortably aestheticized compassion. It appeared only humanitarian that they should become the objects of a powerful social benevolence.

Everywhere "reality" lay open to contest; and everywhere the camera emerged as paradigm for truth. Even James Agee, searching for a literary language that would confront reality in *Let Us Now Praise Famous Men*, refers to the camera as a metaphor for the truth:

all of consciousness is shifted from the imagined, the revisive, to the effort to perceive simply the cruel radiance of what it is. . . . This is why the camera seems to me, next to unassisted and weaponless consciousness, the central instrument of our time. . . . If I could do it I'd do no writing here at all. It would be photographs and the rest would be fragments of cloth, bits of cotton, lumps of earth, records of speeches, pieces of wood and iron, phials of odors, plates of food and excrement. A piece of body torn out by the roots might be more to the point.[16]

Dorothea Lange and Paul Schuster Taylor, *An American Exodus: A Record of Human Erosion*, Reynal & Hitchcock, New York, 1939, pp. 64–5.

That quest which Agee so voraciously pursued overflowed the bounds of the political to permeate every pore of the social body. His urgency to "see" went far beyond the correction of prior misguided myths. Its focus widened to aspects of existence never before visible as sites of passionate intensity. And this imperative to poetically catalog every mundane detail of the Depression's effects signalled the penetration of crisis into the unspeakably intimate.

Yet it is precisely in this intimate penetration that the relation of women to power achieves its complexity. With their access to documentary photography, women took a part in the exercise of power. But as the markers of difference, there is no neutered power on which women can simply lay their hands. A sequence of fictions and masks were invented through which women could be appointed positions.

Documentary was saturated in the values of individuality and equality, key tenets of social democracy. Its understanding was extended, not to the derelict dregs of society, but among individuals equal in their proud humanity. The power of social democracy was never directly open to Dorothea Lange. In relation to documentary's humanism, Lange could be only the "mother," and never "humanity" itself. For "humanity," as seemingly gender neutral term can articulate its norms only through distinction from woman's difference. And in relation to the strained diplomacy of the latter day New Deal, Post Wolcott was specifically named as the charming girl who would unite all parties.

Though each enjoyed her tangential power over truth, the gaze of the camera immediately overturned even these differing positions in power. As instrument of truth, the camera immediately laced a woman's vision with ambivalence, eliding their authorship in a rush to return them to objects of its gaze. The character of their photographs is repeatedly folded back to reveal the photographer as accessible display of womanhood. In the public eye, the meaning of their images was always inflected by the personas

Dorothea Lange. Tenant farmers who have been displaced from their land by tractor farming. Texas.

constructed for the women who had produced them. In relation to the gaze, the position of women is, at the very least, a duality: always simultaneously on both sides of the camera.

Moreover, in their images the women hint at a strength extending beyond this oscillation between positions dictated by a unified I/eye. They sidestep that spectrum that swings from subject of a gaze to she who is subjected to its power. Though in images which were perhaps not widely circulated, they begin to infer an identity which is manifold, and a power in qualities of presence rather than appearance.

The access of "women" to "power" immediately provokes a play in both terms. In relation to a crisis extending into the intimate, a discourse in "power" and the singular positions afforded to "women" insistently slips to reveal multiplicity as its excess.

☐ Documentary did not simply trade on already established feminine stereotypes: be it the compassionate mother that Lange was supposed to embody, the sweet and vivacious girl with whom Post Wolcott was identified, or the unnamed figure who described woman as the locus of desire. To represent the "reality" of the government's benevolence towards its stricken poor, it called forth the fiction of woman as mother. To articulate the "truth" of a united nation returning to prosperity, it called forth the positive image of the energetic young girl.

As a form of enunciation, documentary requires a subject positioned in gender. The I/eye behind the camera becomes distinct and able to address a viewer, through the adoption of sexual difference. The photographer is never neuter, but someone who produces from the place of "man" or "woman." And, like the identity of the subject in language, the gender of the photographer is neither natural nor secure; as the product of repression and artifice, it remains forever precarious.

Documentary called particular notions of the feminine into being, with all the resonance of its pervasive reach. Across its transformation, from classic FSA through positive records to the documentation of war work, a fluidity in gender was set in play. But having been opened to question and thus to change, the identity of gender remained always beyond definitive grasp.

Richard Wright, *12 Million Black Voices: a folk history of the Negro in the United States*, Viking, New York, 1941, p. 74. *Photograph by Marion Post Wolcott.*

☐ The crisis in the regime of truth was not just a sweeping away of anchors in the so called "public" sphere. The process could not stop with dismantling those massively visible social concepts: Economy and Society, Democracy and Class. A crisis in the conception of the real inevitably saturates the most intimate aspects of one's bearings: the ability to daily take up and live, as if entirely natural and safely removed from the social, the positions of "men" and "women." It was not just the identity of the social, but identity in the social which had fractured. Beyond the public clashes of workers and unemployed with police and vigilante armies, the crisis penetrated to less visible and little spoken circuits of power.

One might even say that the interpenetration of these registers of crisis comprised a collapse in the divide between the public and the personal, except that the speech of the decade itself was so insistently social. It so derided this crisis in the intimate that it remained very much a silenced sub-text. Yet the multiple attempts to fix the place of woman forms an undercurrent, just below the surface of this silence, and bears witness to the force of the flux they hoped to contain.

As a speech provoked by a precarious opening in power, and one which hoped to close the question with limited social change, documentary tries to place not only the truth of humanism, but with it the truth of human gender. It is not just a "truth" produced by a gendered I/eye, but a bid to place the I/eye. It tries not only to inhabit the vacuum in authority with its democratic liberalism, but equally to inhabit the home with positions offered in sexuality.

In the FSA work of the mid-1930's, women were repeatedly presented away from social context and in caring relation to their children. In this way, motherhood was removed from historical contingency and made to appear a natural continuity. And this dogged insistence on the Mother is recycled, on another level,[17] in Lange's designation as the mother of her medium. Yet, seen in its relation to an urban audience, this insistence takes on the urgency of repudiation.

Though both men and women suffered staggering levels of unemployment during the Depression, the rate of unemployment in predominantly female jobs was lower than that for men.[18] It had been common for husband and wife to work, though the balance of breadwinning power lay with him; but that very concrete rehearsal of sexual identity was suddenly interrupted. In the face of this most intimate overturning, social reformers from the charitable left to the right campaigned for women to relinquish their jobs and confine themselves to the family.[19]

The incessant picturing of women with their children was never prioritized by Stryker for his photographers; it was not a conscious political device. But perhaps it arose, like the whole of Stryker's enterprise, as part of that widely felt nostalgia for a mythic American past: an American essence as natural as the land, and so located in an immutable rural family. But only for an urban audience could

Esther Bubley. Washington DC 1943.

the land achieve this mythic status, and the rural mother the status of universal touchstone. Perhaps, too, that desire for lost plenitude found in the image of the Mother its most appropriate analogue.

Amongst the other photographic truths vying for ascendancy in the midst of crisis, the truth of gender remained equally uncertain. The cultural left counterposed the individualism of the FSA's poor with the montaged masses of a new class army. Yet its treatment of women remained fraught with contradiction and ambivalence towards change. In awkward proximity to its female militants, it preserved the humanist ideal of woman as natural mother. Its representations thus unwittingly revealed a fissure between change and its containment. And in this overlapping, it made present an untenable simultaneity of femininities.

Photographed for strike sheets and trade union journals, women appeared on picket lines either alongside men, or in poses ritually struck by men before them. Their presence as women went almost without notice; but not because class militancy has assuaged the division of the sexes and forged a unique androgyny. Visually, and therefore politically, they were subsumed within conventions which had marked militancy as a male preserve. To become visible as militant, women were effectively made masculine. In this, their transformation was, given articulate space and simultaneously rendered silent.

Alongside the militancy of the unions and of the organized unemployed, many groupings attempted social change on the cultural rather than economic level. Through work in the theater, in music, literature and the visual arts, they attempted to forge a fighting proletarian culture. Amongst those devoted specifically to a politics in culture, women were again formally accepted as equals. But in the emergent medium of photomontage, they appear, again imperceptably, amongst the embattled crowds; and where an individual is montaged as exemplary leader of that action, it is *he* who invariably vaunts his herculean brawn.[20] Cameos of both men and women, injured in the course of struggle, are inset alongside the crowds. But where the man is displayed as he fought, ragged, bandaged and bloody, the woman appears in untouched portrait—still somehow the unruffled object of a gaze.[21] Where individual women are given the breadth of a full page image, it is amongst their children as martyred mothers, wives of imprisoned "class warriors."

The need to continually re-place the feminine belies a confusion and a tension surrounding sexual difference. The need to masculinize the woman militant, and yet to preserve her difference as mother and as seen; the need to repeatedly perfect an icon of rural motherhood before an audience in the city hint intriguingly at slippages away from the place of the feminine. Far from fixing women's social position, they endlessly return us to a crisis in the truth of gender.

☐ Reality, as proposed by documentary, was not only one of bald fact, but of fact informed by human feeling. Within its own discourse, it was precisely the element of compassion which elevated documentary above mere empirical research. Yet, paradoxically, this appeal to emotional engagement potentially cast suspicion on its claim to dispassionate realism.

But documentary resided as much in the talking and the writing which invested its practise with meaning as in its images; and much of its discourse was devoted to smoothing this seeming contradiction. Statement upon statement defines the countervailing demands of science and compassion, and then attempts to render them legible as coherence.

Stryker himself was a prominent architect of documentary as both objective and impassioned reality: "simple honesty will render to the pictures the dignity of fact; feeling and insight will give their fraction of a second's exposure the integrity of truth."[22] And this dichotomy was elaborated again and again across the expanding range of amateur journals and public symposia on photography. An editorial of *The Complete Photographer* argued that "To distinguish between documentary and other kinds of photography, let's say that the documentary photographer adds to the personal factor of self-expression the social factor of 'historian in pictures' ..."[23] And Berenice Abbott, a photographer employed under the New Deal's Works Progress Administration, makes a similar point to a conference of women on photography: "There is a sociological value to documentary photography ... yet the plus which makes the difference between statistics and an expressive statement is that sense of life."[24]

As a conference specifically for women, the discussion subsequent to Abbott's remarks began to glimpse the interplay between the divisions in documentary and a crisis that had fractured accepted notions of the feminine. Documentary attempted to disperse its internal differences across a divide in sexuality, allotting to women a privilege over feeling and to men the authority over facts. It attempted not only to fix a reality torn between science and compassion, but in so doing to fix a troubling flux in sexuality. The discourse of documentary thus became a site at which two registers of social crisis were interwoven. The instability in documentary's reality was articulated across an instability in the intimate arena of gender. And the dichotomy in documentary became a site at which the masculine and feminine could be redefined.

At the women's conference on photography, the speaker from the US Film Service claimed women's "interest in the human problem" as their means to overcome resistance to their entry into the field. She thought it the key to the success enjoyed by both Lange and Post Wolcott, the only two women thus far acclaimed for their FSA work.[25] And perhaps inadvertently, she directly echoed the terms in which Stryker had distinguished Lange, in her humanity, from the accuracy of Walker Evans:

'I respected Walker's pictures for their almost medical precision, their great skill, but they were cool ... then Dorothea's work came in. I hadn't even met her yet, but ... I saw a sense—the Mother— the great feeling for human beings she had which was so valuable. She could go into the field and a man working there would look up, and he must have had some feeling that there was a wonderful woman, and that she was going to be sympathetic, and this never failed to show in her work.'[26]

Such was the power of association of woman with feeling and man with authority over facts that the photographers themselves internalized them as integral to their practice. In interview, Edwin and Louise Rosskam, husband and wife who both photographed for the FSA, differentiated their practices thus:

ER: ... it has, because it was a mechanical process, that particular credibility that all the novels in the world could not command. It has an air of fact ...

LR: ... when I got a camera into my hands ... I wanted to get people to understand how that woman holding that child, without enough to eat, felt; and I waited until I took the picture—til the ultimate of her emotions seemed to show, and then quickly got the picture ... I wanted to feel that, and get other people to feel it.'[27]

In her choice of the mother and child as paradigm for feeling, Louise Rosskam trades on both Lange's appellation as Mother of documentary, and Lange's image of the Migrant Mother, which had quickly become representative of her entire oeuvre. In her brief statement, the rhetoric of woman as receptacle of feeling, which had been aimed at the women photographers, met the rhetoric of woman as mother, which had been aimed at the photographs' subjects.

Louise and Edwin Rosskam argued out the dichotomy of documentary within their intimate relation. Their positions, as posed within the debate between fact and feeling, immediately became their positions in sexual identity. And the debate over documentary became embroiled in the endless attempt to hold the tenuous terrain of gender.

☐ Though understood as the receptacles of feeling, each woman photographer was nonetheless positioned through a precise and differing emotionality. In hailing Lange as the "Mother," Stryker placed her as the mirror of the immutable motherhood that many of her photographs would subsequently suggest. Her consuming empathy for her subjects became synonymous with her subject's caring for their children. Though only a fraction of her images conformed to the transcendent ideal of mother and child, it was the image of the Migrant Mother which soared to the status of icon, and became the hallmark of Lange herself.

The naming of Lange as 'Mother' folded across the reading of her images. It not only prioritized certain images, but became intimately embedded in the sense that could be made of them. The reading across them of a natural humanity gained momentum through reference to her as a paradigm for a caring humanism. And likewise, her compassionate persona was repeatedly reinforced by the appeal her photographs articulated on the part of the rural poor.

Through such readings of her images, Lange's characterization became pivotal in the broader political discourse of social democracy. In the crisis of truth and power which marked the Depression, the belief in a nation benevolent to its citizens ultimately held sway over the collectivity of class. In the meeting of the many documentaries produced on the left and right, it was the proud individual of the FSA photographs who came out in the ascendancy. But the putting into place of the "truth" of humanism rested inextricably on the putting into place of "truths" of human gender. The bid to describe the crisis as reparable through American resilience immediately entailed claims on the identities of Lange, Evans and their subjects as essentially American men and women.

Such was the mythology around Lange's strength of feeling that her personal testament, alone, became a guarantee of truth: she had achieved the rare status of trusted eye-witness, whose mere presence behind the camera ensured that reality had been revealed. Paradoxically, however, the continual

Richard Wright, *12 Million Black Voices*. Photograph by Dorothea Lange.

re-securing of that status meant that the discourse around her photographs gradually shifted from the photographed subject to her as conduit of their enduring humanity; her own humanity was interchanged with theirs.

To accompany a series of Lange's pictures in *US Camera*, Pare Lorentz[28] produced a text entitled "Searching, Seeking, Sorrowing, Pictures That Tell the 'Okie' Story"; but his emphasis is as much on Lange herself as on the pictured migrants: "Dorothea Lange is a little, soft-voiced bright eyed woman with a weather beaten face who, for six years, beret cocked over one ear, has been stalking the back roads of the country photographing the poor ... your Texans and Okies and Southern Highlanders are proud people. They do not like you to invade their privacy, poverty-stricken though it may be. Yet they trust a chattering little woman with a camera slung over her shoulder on sight, and not because she is earnest and deeply interested in them as people, rather than as photographic subjects—but because she is one of them."[29]

The interchangeability of her humanity with theirs guaranteed the classless equality of social democracy. Through a mother's compassion for each person, she isolated her subjects and removed them from social context. Her photographs offer us the alluring pleasure of intimate contact. Their subjects' integrity seems to mirror our own. Their suffering was transformed from the product of social crisis to an eternal human dilemma; and so was accompanied by the majesty of man's great enduring

142

"WE AIN'T NO PAUPERS. WE HOLD OURSELVES TO BE WHITE FOLKS. WE DON'T WANT NO RELIEF. WHAT WE DO WANT IS A CHANST TO MAKE AN HONEST LIVING LIKE WHAT WE WAS RAISED"

110

U.S. Camera, v. 1: "America," 1941, pp. 110–11. *Photographs by Dorothea Lange.* (Courtesy of U.S. Camera Imnc.)

"WE GOT TROUBLES ENOUGH WITHOUT GOING COMMUNIST"

144

sentiments. All structural social division was levelled before this equality in human essence.

In this sense her characterization as the Mother of documentary became the crucial platform from which political benevolence could issue. And her images could be mobilized in a liberal polemic against "impersonal" left-wing "dogma":

Her people stand straight and look you in the eye. They have the simple dignity of people who have leaned against the wind, and worked in the sun and owned their own land.... Wherever she goes she brings back people.... Not only will Lange bring back people, but she'll bring them back without any tricks. Where so many earnest young men try to get a portrait, a social viewpoint, an economic study, all in one picture, she only tries to show you a human being. There is in her work none of the left-wing self conscious social irony that so often defeats the purpose of creative workmen with a point of view.[30]

Her images invest our gaze with the power of compassion; and though industrious, her subjects invest in the authorities power over their rescue. A report on migrants in photos and text, which she produced with Paul Taylor for the reforming journal *Survey Graphic* ascribed to them this helplessness: "... to many people the Depression has brought collapse so complete and so protracted that they cannot rise by themselves to survive."[31] Taylor goes on to support the success of the migrant camps, not only in alleviating distress, but in deflecting radical self-organization amongst the migrants: "since they are designed to demonstrate more decent living conditions, they will remove one of the most fruitful causes of unrest and strongest supports of agitation."[32]

In the discourse of Lange as Mother, and in the repeated use of her family shots, an entire politics is constructed around the individual, tradition and the family. In another collaboration with Lange, Taylor construes destitute migrants in the tradition of the American pioneers, going west in covered wagons: "Thus the refugees seeking *individual* protection in the *traditional* spirit of the American frontier by westward migration are unknowingly arrivals at another frontier, that of social unrest. ... A family of refugees in dire distress naturally helped to break the strike. With the earnings they purchased an automobile badly needed for *family* support" (my emphasis).[33] The family is summoned as intrinsic value whose destruction is threatened by social change.

Lange's placement as mother thus came to underpin not only a refusal of social conflict, but a conservative nostalgia for the myth of a shared American past.

☐ Where Lange had allegedly been the Mother, documentary attempted to cast Post Wolcott as its "girl." And where Lange's difference was vaunted through her depth of compassion, Post Wolcott's was marked through a demonstrative frisson around her unorthodox travels alone in the field. Her entire public persona was provoked through a play on the dangers she faced, thus covertly insisting on sexuality and transgression. Though her fearlessness was always the object of ostensible admiration, the continual evocation of the dangers eroticized her presence as, itself, an invitation.

In reminiscing about his photographers, Stryker reiterated his admiration for "Dorothea" as the "Mother." When he came to Post Wolcott, however, he commented briefly on her "great sense of our land" and "feeling of people on the land" but then proceeded to the vulnerability and the bravura surrounding her sexuality: "Marion also suffered from being a very attractive girl, and I always wondered how she could get along. The war was just starting, and I asked Marion one time, I said 'Marion, don't you have some trouble around sometimes.' She said, 'Yes, very often a local policeman picks me up. We have Coke, and he asks me something about my sex life, and I ask him about his, and by this time I look at my watch and say "If I don't get back to work I'm going to get fired!"' '"[34]

The intrigue of her transgression was far from Stryker's private affair. The *Washington Post* headed an article on her travels with "Girl Photographer for FSA Travels 50,000 Miles in Search for Pictures. It takes considerable courage, not to mention credentials galore, to venture into the hinterlands with a camera these days—particularly when you are a comely young girl."[35] And transcribing this drama into a contemporary context, Post Wolcott's brief biographical sketch in the only FSA bibliography takes the space to tell us that Post Wolcott carried a hatchet in her suitcase.[36]

The resilient girlishness constructed in her place became a pivot round which she could move into a more positive and hopeful photographic practise, quite distinct from Lange's. By the time Post Wolcott was taken on in 1938, Stryker was under pressure to justify the expense of the FSA's rural resettlement programs. "I think my role was a little different from the earlier photographers. I was given a lot of gaps to fill in ... Roy, at the time I came in, wanted pictures of lush America, ... more 'canned goods' of the FSA positive remedial programs."[37] "My occasional emphasis on pretty pictures showing the beauty, strength and fertility of the land and the successes of the FSA programs, was calculated to win the hearts of many in Congress ... I believed my photographs might help to overcome or counteract the opposition in influential and wealthy landowners, plantation owners, and members of the Farm Bureau who were afraid of the effects of 'radical, social, communistic' programs."[38]

As the only new full-time staff photographer, charged alone with this redirection of the photographic project, Post Wolcott—like Lange—played a crucial role in transforming documentary practise. Yet, it was a role in which the difference of her gender had been far from neutralized; for her youthful capacity to charm became a cipher for her photographs' capacity to placate. She was positioned in documentary not despite of, but partially because of her difference. Moreover, the transition she negotiated in documentary equally marked a change in woman's difference, and consequently in the truth of the feminine. And the meanings attributed to her femininity were continually evoked as sub-text, reiterated across the readings of her images.

Although her work by no means conformed to her anodyne brief,[39] that which was lent the greatest force appeared as parts of the new eulogies to both the American small town[40] and to the land. As the country mobilized for war, Post Wolcott's images filled the pages of *Fair Is Our Land*,[41] a pictorial essay which sought "to portray the beauty of the American countryside, at a time when the preservation of this fair land, and all it stands for, is uppermost in the minds of all Americans."[42] The land itself had become the site around which national unity might be forged, and the value which that nation had at stake.

Like Lange's work, Post Wolcott's images were used to overcome or even pre-empt potential social conflict. But where in Lange's work the site of that cohesion was human dignity, transcending circumstances and suffering, in Post Wolcott's work it is the revelation of an essential national character in its landscape. Visually removed from the actual centers of social conflict, landscape *as symbol* could be laden with connotations of an American essence which had been shared—perhaps imperceptibly— by all the contesting parties. Yet the difficulty of achieving unification remained manifest in lengthy refusals of past social division:

146

Five Million Barrels of cement were required to build Boulder Dam on the Colorado River in Western United States. Constructed to hold back the river's flood torrents, this dam is the highest in the world, rising 726 feet above bedrock. It irrigates vast areas, furnishes cheap electric power.

Roaring Blast Furnaces spew out flame and smoke as America girds herself for war. The United States produces twice as much steel as any other country in the world: 82,836,946 tons in 1941 against Germany's 24,700,000 tons. Steel plants all over the country are running on a 24-hour-a-day basis.

Victory, v. 1 n. 1, pp. 6–7.

New York City After Dark. Thousands of lights dot the huge skyscrapers, making a fairyland of the teeming metropolis that houses over 7,000,000 people and is the commercial center of the world. The lighted structure in the upper left of the picture is the 70-story, 850-feet-tall RCA building.

A Parkway Near New York, one of the superb highways that link all important U. S. cities. This one is the Grand Central Parkway. Capable of holding six cars abreast at some points, these magnificent roads are designed for the safety and comfort of millions of American motorists.

148

Tobacco Field in the Kentucky Mountains *Marion Post Wolcott for F.S.A.*

Contrasting Farms in Kentucky – The Backwoods *Marion Post Wolcott for F.S.A.*

Tobacco Harvest *Marion Post Wolcott for F.S.A.*
70
FAIR IS OUR LAND

Dairy Farm in Jefferson County – Kentucky *Marion Post Wolcott for F.S.A.*
THE FARM
71

Samuel Chamberlain (ed.), *Fair Is Our Land: The Portrait of America*, Hastings House, New York, pp. 70–1. (Courtesy of Hasting House). *Photographs by Marion Post Wolcott.*

In recent years a deafening babble has been dinning at our ears, striking doubt and despair in all but the strongest hearts. The voices have come hurling at us from all directions: the shriek of headlines pitched to shock us into buying two cents' worth of vicarious sensation; the oily voice of radio, selling scented optimism and patriotism by the tube; the jingo's boastful shout, the warning shot of myopic little men called isolationists; the suave tones of government and the empty rumble of powerful interests; the defiant clamor of labor; the voice of Youth, cruelly mistaught to demand its "rights" to something for nothing; the crabbed voice of Age, begging sanctuary; and for a background, the sound of money changing hands.

Amidst this dismissal of those who provoke division in the nation, an attempt is made to recuperate unity:

Listening to the loud claims and easy promises, it was easy to lose sight of the country's innate capacity for good sense and goodwill, and to forget how, sadly, the public accents were mistaken for the private voice of America.[43]

The voice of America was no longer that of the New Deal's social welfare for the defenseless, but one of a powerful destiny: "... this is the great American virtue, this American Dream: faith in our mastery of the future."[44] Post Wolcott's positive images played a crucial part in thus aligning the power of the land with the power of the nation.

☐ Post Wolcott's images were authenticated as truth, though their rhetoric was substantially different from those of the mid-1930's. By the time most of the women entered documentary practise, however, that status of truth had become more ambiguous. During wartime, there was no discourse around either the photographers or their products to parallel that which placed Lange and Post Wolcott publicly. When the images appeared in the publications of the Office of War Information, they appeared without bylines; so, in a sense, the photographers' status as authors had been lost. And because they appeared in organs of war propaganda, their credibility as truth is difficult to ascertain.

The OWI produced a series of periodicals and leaflets, which were banned from distribution in the US, or to American civilian or military personnel overseas. They were aimed, then, at winning the loyalty of Europeans, especially in the Axis countries. In America, and in an American-led world, they would find freedom through modern industrialized civilization. Images vaunted American power through monumental cityscapes, vast looping networks of highways, the monolithic structures of industry, and the towering formations of the land. Yet America remained nonetheless a land of religious and family values, echoing those of its readership. Image and text return continually to the cohesion and democracy of the American small town.

The role of sexual difference in making the meaning of these images remains, for us, invisible. To understand something of the placing of the feminine within this photographic practise, our only recourse then is to our own fascination with the images. Through the fragmentary frames of meaning that ensue, we attempt to place not only the world within the photograph, but ourselves as fragmentary subjects.

It is tempting to track the feminine in this sequence: Lange as the "mother," Post Wolcott as the "girl," through to the later photographs where the urban woman becomes a locus of desire. Even in this linear progression, they display a fluid femininity, and so constitute a firm rebuttal (if one was needed) of any essentialist dream. Yet they still preserve the feminine in any given moment as a unity, thus underwriting our own longing for such coherence. And the succession of each model after the last implies the supercession of all three by a self-congratulating "modern woman."

But in the writing, these models cannot exist in sequence, but simultaneously, inconsistently, in the present. Their legibility for us consists in their persistence; or, more to the point, the writing calls up the persistence of each, in parallel, into its present. In relation to the documents presented by the archive, we construe these places of the feminine inevitably in terms of their contemporary legibility; across their gaps we play out our contemporary incoherences. They become the protagonists of a contemporary fiction: not the history of the present, but history in the present.

Though instrumental as a structure, this marking of positions and positions in sequence, can only give rise to its excess. (The mark always belies the space outside its perimeter.) The images cannot sustain their authors as unified points of origin any more than they can sustain us as unified points of arrival. Their announcement is not of the viewer's arrival at one vantage point but of our incitement in diverse directions.

Dorothea Lange. Daughter of a migrant Tennessee coal miner living in American River Camp. Sacramento, California (vicinity). November 1936.

☐ In 1936, Lange produced an image which she captioned 'Daughter of a migrant Tennessee coal miner, living in American River Camp'. Her sorrow seems to float in nowhere. She is present only through a face and hand which emerge, blanched white, from the darkness: fragments embraced within soft gradations of velvety black. She might at one level confirm the mythic figure of the woman of darkness: woman shrouded in mystery: the enigma who, when investigated, gives over to terror and the frozen gaze of fetishism. For these severed aspects of her body—a hand sliced at the wrist, a head underlined at the neck—appear as ready sites for potential disavowal.

Lange as the Mother would inevitably guarantee the place of the Father, and thus his gaze. The immediacy of compassionate contact, which marked her view as the Mother's, nonetheless rested on inciting an appropriating gaze. With the intimacy of knowing the needs of the poor, went the ascendancy of a benevolent viewer over those helplessly observed. Speaking the needs of the poor *for* them, her images provoke the pleasure of perusing a passive object. Even where Lange shows women as mothers, desire in the gaze persists. It is the operation of fetishism which permits the directness of our contact and the fixity of both our position and theirs. For, in the retrospective fictions we weave around our pasts, the mother is after all the originary site/sight of castrating terror; contact with her can only be re-established on the basis of disavowal. Even in the now archetypal image of the Migrant Mother, the

Dorothea Lange. Daughter of migrant Tennessee coal miner living in American River Camp. Sacramento, California (vicinity). November 1936.

children take up this function of the mother's stand-in phallus. They save us the fear of her absence and so make safe the assuring illusion of her presence.

As "daughter," this woman might similarly have been placed on the axis of woman as other—daughter, wife, mother—and seen in a similar light. And in the absence of any sign of her social circumstances, her sorrow might—like the Migrant Mother—have incited our transcendent shared humanity. But in many ways she becomes more than this. She becomes impossible to locate in space. Realism is undermined by the surface use of black, pierced only by head and hand. And her unfocussed gaze presents further obfuscation. Sorrow seems to add to this drift away from position, re-mapping the body as site for her fantasized dispersion. Had she been old, lined and weathered, that head in that hand might have itself constituted a basis for pity's power; but her youth, even her beauty, constitute a problem for that reading. The light seems to caress and articulate the contours of her face. Through her sensuality, her own resources insist; and intrigue is added to her unrealized reverie.

A similar image of the same young woman was printed in the reforming journal *Shelter*, alongside the article "Hovels in the Miners Call Home" (October 1938). But there, the camera had taken greater distance to emphasize the dishevelled cot on which she sat within her tent. There, her sorrow was tied down to destitution, and her place tied down to her hovel. There, she became the object of potential amelioration, her sensuous presence overridden with powerless need.

Marion Post Wolcott. Advertisement on the side of a drugstore window. Wendell, North Carolina. 1939.

But here, in the image that was never used, there is a quiet strength about the pose. She is not collapsed in dereliction; neither has she that hard bitten strength of years "leaning against the wind." She does not present the dogged heroism of those surviving at the lowest level: a heroism easily granted to those over which one ultimately has power.

Though now bemused, there is a sense that she once believed in other possibilities. And there is a sense that, in Lange's appreciation of that other presence, Lange approached her not entirely as the knowing Mother, but also as a woman of equal complexity. In the disparate fictions made possible by her image, Lange exceeds the constraints of one position and so provokes in us a difference in selves.

☐ In accordance with her assignment to the American small town, Post Wolcott produced a street scene in the town of Wendell, North Carolina in 1939. A white man stands staunch, blunt, even challenging in his posture. A white woman clutches her infant protectively as she passes along the street behind him. And behind her, two black men swerve to keep their distance, the length of their gait lending urgency to their avoidance.

The white man's stance is intractable; the black men hurry to defer: though they remain free to move, theirs is the scurrying mobility of the powerless. The men's postures lucidly diagram a crude differential in power, in which the woman is caught as a conduit. The clutching of the child seems to speak the woman's own vulnerability, in her position poised between two threats. Her frozen step, unlike the white man's stillness, makes her hesitant, and so attributes even to the black men a relative power in their physical mobility.[50]

We strain for the detail of these complexly layered interactions, but are kept at frustrating distance. The shot is captioned "Advertisement on the side of a drug store," suitable subject for a positive small town document; and the camera is positioned as if this were its only subject. As a result, the image offers us two relations, forever interchanging with one another. The idiosyncratic imagery of small town commerce remains obscured—perhaps even scarred—by the tensions of the street. So the I/eye oscillates from romanticized small trade to an exchange of power at the site of a woman.

Esther Bubley. 1943.

And Bubley's woman in her boarding house bedroom returns us to that ambiguity of position opened by the woman in her car. She shares in that unfocussed reverie, and so in that tilt from presence through its excess. The image shares in that modulation of surface, and so directs us again from desire through to fantasy. Where the gaze might have attempted to position and possess her, it becomes mobile amongst fragments of the image. She looks away, and so disperses the gaze from knowledge through a drift. Yet the oscillation is not an innocent one between the desire of our gaze and the desires of her reverie. For she cannot become the locus of desire without inciting an ambivalence of her own.

The portrait of Mum and Dad stands as comforting reminder on the dressing table top. But a wide angle lens has placed her as apex of a disorienting distortion. In the door frame nearest to Mum and Dad, a sullen figure is obscured in the darkness, only her hand ominously intruding into the bedroom. As the author of this collision, doors and mirrors tilt away from her as desire's unstable hub. In the turning of her face from the truths of home, the image fragments into multiple scenes: tokens of identity in confusion. Amidst the precarious play of her own desires, the intruding hand threatens. It poses a crisis in the uniform surface of the image, and thus a crisis in the intimate space of her longings: but is this a danger posed to her, or simply that posed by new desires to the order of her past?

Notes

This material was initially gathered preliminary to the production of a PhD thesis at the University of Leeds.

1. Marie Yates, "Image/Woman/Text," *Issue: Social Strategies by Woman Artists*, 1980, catalogue to the exhibition selected by Lucy Lippard for the Institute of Contemporary Arts, London.

2. Jean François Lyotard, "Adrift," *Driftworks*, New York, Semiotext(e), Inc., p. 16.

3. Laura Mulvey, "Visual Pleasure and the Narrative Cinema," *Screen*, Vol. 16, No. 3, 1975, pp. 6–7.

4. Lyotard, op. cit., p. 10.

5. Laura Mulvey, "Notes on Sirk and Melodrama," *Movie*, No. 25, 1977, p. 56.

6. Lyotard, op. cit., p. 10.

7. Julia Kristeva, "Women's Time," *Signs*, Vol. 7, No. 1, 1981.

8. Mary Anne Doane, "Women's Stake: Filming the Female Body," *October*, No. 17, 1981, pp. 28–9.

9. Jane Gallop, *Feminism and Psychoanalysis: The Daughter's Seduction*, Macmillan, London, 1982, p. xiii.

10. Elizabeth Cowie, "Fantasia," *m/f*, No. 9, 1984, pp. 71–4.

11. Michel Foucault, *The Archaeology of Knowledge*, translated by A. M. Sheridan Smith, Tavistock, London, 1972, p. 14.

12. Dorothea Lange contributed to the file from 1935 to 1939, Marion Post Wolcott from 1938 to 1942, Louise Rosskam from 1940 to 1943, Martha Macmillan during 1941, Marjorie Collins from 1942–1943, Pauline Ehrlich during 1944, Ann Rosener from 1942 to 1943, and Esther Bubley from 1941 to 1943

13. *One of Esther Bubley's images is reproduced in Roy Stryker and Nancy Woods, In This Proud Land: America, 1935–1945, as seen in the FSA Photographs* but is passed over without mention in the text.

14. In 1938, photographs which Walker Evans had taken for the FSA were presented alone by the Museum of Modern Art in New York under the title "American Photographs." And in 1936 and 1939, Berenice Abbott's pictures of New York, taken as documentary for the Work Progress Administration under the New Deal, appeared in Museum of Art exhibitions entitled "New Horizons in American *Art*" and "*Art* of Our Time."

15. William Stott, *Documentary Expression and Thirties America*, Oxford University Press, New York, 1973, pp. 78–9.

16. James Agee and Walker Evans, *Let Us Now Praise Famous Men*, Houghton Mifflin, Boston, 1929, reprinted 1980, p. 11 and p. 13.

17. For more extensive discussion see W. Kozol, "The Ideology of Gender and the Farm Security Administration," unpublished thesis, 1985, UCLA.

18. Ruth Milkman, "Women's Work and Economic Crises: Some Lessons of the Great Depression," *Review of Radical Political Economy*, Vol. 8, No. 1, 1976, pp. 75–7.

19. For example, cover *Labor Defender: America's Only Labor Pictorial*, February 1934.

20. Ibid., "1,250,000," April 1930.

21. Ibid.

22. R. Stryker, "Documentary Photography," *Popular Photography*, No. 21, 1942.

23. Editorial: "Documentary Photography," *The Complete Photographer*, No. 21, 1942.

158

24. Berenice Abbott, address entitled "Civic Documentary History" to the Conference on Photography held by the Institute of Women's Professional Relations, New York City, 9 February 1940.

25. In his address to the Conference, Stryker actively discouraged women from picture making for "lack of opportunity," and encouraged them instead to edit the written and pictorial reports in which the photographs appeared. His own office employed many women in this behind the scenes capacity. See FSA papers, Box 5: Personnel, on microfilm at the Library of Congress.

26. *Just Before the War: Urban America from 1935 to 1941 as seen by photographers of the FSA*. Catalog of the exhibition at the Newport Art Museum and the Library of Congress, October House, New York, 1968.

27. Edwin and Louise Rosskam, interviewed by Richard K. Doud, 3 August 1965, Roosevelt New Jersey, transcript with Archive of American Art, Washington DC.

28. Pare Lorentz was named motion picture consultant to the Resettlement Administration information staff in 1935. He remained in charge of the film unit after its transfer to the Farm Security Administration in 1937, and was later to head the United States Film Service.

29. Pare Lorentz, "Searching, Seeking, Sorrowing, Pictures That Tell the 'Okie' Story," *US Camera*, Vol. I, 1941.

30. Ibid.

31. Paul Taylor, "From the Ground Up," *Survey Graphic*, March 1936.

32. Ibid.

33. Paul Taylor, "Again the Covered Wagon," *Survey Graphic*, July 1935.

34. Roy Stryker, interviewed by Richard K. Doud, 17 October 1963, transcript in the Archive of American Art, Washington DC.

35. J. Brownell, "Girl Photographer for FSA Travels 50,000 Miles in Search for Pictures," *Washington Post*, 19 November 1940. A piece of a similar nature appeared in *PM's Weekly*, 17 August 1941.

36. Penelope Dixon, *Photographers of the Farm Security Administration: An Annotated Bibliography 1930–1980*, Garland, 1983.

37. Marion Post Wolcott, interviewed by Richard K. Doud, 18 January 1965, transcript with Archive of American Art, Washington DC.

38. Marion Post Wolcott, "FSA—My Role," unpublished contemporary statement.

39. See S. Stein, "Marion Post Wolcott: Thoughts on Some Lesser Known FSA Photographs," *Marion Post Wolcott: FSA Photographs*, Friends of Photography, Carmel, California, 1983, on her attention to tensions around race and class, primarily in the South.

40. Sherwood Anderson, *Home Town*, Alliance, New York, 1940.

41. Samuel Chamberlain (ed.), *Fair Is Our Land*, Hastings House, New York, 1942.

42. Ibid., Editor's note.

43. Ibid., Introduction by Daniel Moffat.

44. Ibid.

45. See Stein, op. cit., for discussion of this image in relation to the positions white women *vis-à-vis* race politics. Alleged attacks on white women formed the most frequent justification for lynchings; yet white women played a crucial role in lobbying for anti-lynching laws through the Association of Southern Women for the Prevention of Lynching.

Arthur Rothstein. Grand Central Station. New York, New York. 1941.